FOOD *for the* MASSES

LYRICS & PORTRAITS

"We can bomb the world to pieces
but we can't bomb it into peace."
—Michael Franti

(cover image) Michael says, "Good night y'all," at the Ancienne Belgique. Brussels, Belgium, 2001

(previous page) Performing at Pink Pop festival in Holland, 2001

MICHAEL FRANTI

FOOD *for the* MASSES

LYRICS & PORTRAITS

Photography by WONDER KNACK

INSIGHT
EDITIONS

CONTENTS

Performing at Berbati's Pan, Portland, Oregon, 2000

(overleaf) Original draft of "Speaking of Tongues," 2000

A STRANGE STRANGE LITANY OF VERSES
AND REVERSES
AD LIBS AND REHEARSES
CLOUDS BURST AND WORDS CURSED
AN ARGUMENT BREAKS OUT
IT'S ONE WE'VE ALL HEARD BEFORE
ITS BORING HAD US ALL SNORING
FROM THE FIRST LINE
ONE AFTER ANOTHER CHIMED IN PERFECT TIME
TIRED REHASHES AND PETTY CASHES AND MISMATCHES
YOU SHOULDA COULDA'S AND WHY
DIDN'T YA DIDA'S
CRIPPLING SNIPPETS AIMED AT THE HEART
TO INFLAME AND IMPART BLAME
FRAMED LIKE MUMIA
VERBAL DIARRHEA
SPASMS CREATING CHASMS
BETWEEN THE SOULS OF TWO
OR TWO BILLION
NATIONS TORN APART
STATION TO STATION DAMNATION
WITH MUCH DELIBERATION
AND VERY LITTLE CONSIDERATION
TO THE RETURN ON THE DAMAGE
FROM THE ALTERCATION
COLLATERAL CONDEMNATION
THEN DENYIN' LIKE COLORIZATION
OF AN OLD BLACK & WHITE

CREATE A REVISION OF THE RECENT LAST
NIGHT
THE FIGHT THAT STARTED WITH TWO
WORDS... "I'M RIGHT"
OF COURSE THE FIGHT ENDS WITH NO
RESOLUTION
MERELY A VOW FOR RETRIBUTION
SUBSTITUTION, EXECUTION, ELECTROCUTION.
RUTHLESS, TRUTHLESS AND TOOTHLESS
MUMBLING. THROUGH PAGE AFTER PAGE
OF EXCUSES
ABUSES OF THE GIFT OF GAB
GABRIEL THE TRUMPETER BESTOWED
UPON US A VOICE WITH A CHOICE
AND A TONGUE KEPT MOIST BY
YEARS OF SALIVATING AFTER
FOR OYSTERS PEARLS AND AFRODESIACS
LOCKED IN AN UGLY SHELL
ALWAYS TO CHEWEY AN GOOEY
SO THEY GET SWALLOWED WHOLE
BUT A TONGUE IS SO MUCH MORE
THAN A VEHICLE FOR GREED
OF THE DECIPHERER OF FEED
A TONGUE IS FOR WASHING FUR
OR FOR LICKING WOUNDS
OR WELCOMING NEWCOMERS INTO A RO
OR CLEANSING THOSE FRESH FROM THE WO

WITHOUT A TONGUE THERE'D BE NO
CROONS SWOONS JUNES UNDER THE MOONS
NO BEES POLLINATIN NO FLOWERS TO BLOOM
NO RESITATION OF WORDS AT THE FOOT
OF A TOMB
OR WILLS READ ALLOWED OF THE FAMILY
HEIRLOOMS
YOU PROBABLY COULDN'T EVEN BLOW
UP A BALLOON
AND THAT WOULD BE A SHAME
BECAUSE TO EXHALES THE NAME
OF THE GAME
EXHALE FROM THE HEART
NOT FROM THE LUNGS
SPEAK FROM THE HEART, NOT
FROM THE TONGUE!

"LISTENING" IS UNDERSTANDING
AND FINDING COMPASSION
"LOVE" IS THE ACTION OF SOUL SATISFACTION
A TONGUE CAN MAKE WISHES
AND ALSO FINE KISSES
TASTE A SWEET CAKE AND ALSO
CAST DISSES
BUT NOTHIN' COMPARES TO THE
VOICE FROM WITHIN
WITHOUT WE MIGHT JUST BE
MANNEQUINS

UP TO NO DARN GOOD SHENANIGANS
LEARN TO BE SKILLFUL MOVERS
~~SKILLFUL MOVERS~~ OF THE STONES
THAT BLOCK THE HEART
AND TURNS HUMANS TO CLONES
LEARN TO FORGIVE AND SET FREE
THE BONES
TOUCH WITH YOUR FLESH
TAKE OFF THE RUBBER GLOVES
LOVE LIKE YOUR LIFE DEPENDS
ON IT, BECAUSE IT DOES

INTRODUCTION / MICHAEL FRANTI

I am equally committed to music, social justice and making people laugh and it is from this place that all my lyrics are written.

If there is one common theme that runs through the body of my work it is compassion. Finding love in our hearts for ourselves and in turn trying to find empathy for the lives of others. This is not an easy task. There is so much to find wrong with the world we live in. You don't have to look far to find injustice, pain, greed and sorrow. In fact the overabundance of these things leads us to look the other way, a vain attempt to tune out the world around us.

I write songs to tune in.

To tune into the voice of our hearts. Tune into the fear, frustration, sadness and elation of ourselves or someone we've never met before. Tune into emotions inside of us we never new existed until we heard the opening chords of Bill Withers "Lean On Me" or the growl in Marvin Gaye's voice on "Mercy, Mercy Me (the Ecology)," the urgency of Bob Marley's "Get Up, Stand Up," or the poignancy of John Lennon's "Imagine."

I don't write because I enjoy it (although I do), I don't write because I hope others will enjoy it (although I hope they will).

I write because I need to. Because if I did not have this vehicle of expression I would lose my mind. It is my desire that my songs serve a similar purpose for those who enjoy them. To help others make sense of their unexpressed feelings about the world.

I believe all creativity comes from the same spirit. It is our ability to remain open to that spirit that enables it to pass through our brush onto the easel, our words to the paper, or from our kitchens to the table.

I wish I had a perfect formula to tap into this energy all the time...but alas, I have yet to find one. This book represents years of my struggle to turn my thoughts into delectable fruit, the seeds of which might take hold in the hearts of those who are hungry for it.

I hope that *Food for the Masses* will bring longtime listeners fresh insight into familiar songs and will introduce newcomers to a body of work that has now spanned nearly two decades.

Thanks for all the support you have given me over the years. I hope you enjoy the lyrics as much as I have enjoyed writing them.

Michael at the Sugar Shack, San Francisco, 2002

THE BEATNIGS

1986

NATURE

SITTIN IN THE GREEN GRASS
WATCHIN THE STRANGE WORLD OF ANTS
Do Their Dance
NATURE
AT THE BEACH
WATCHIN Rocks smash into Pebbles
AND whisper into sand
in my hands
AND PEOPLE OFTEN ASK ME
MICHAEL?
IF YOU LOVE NATURE SO MUCH

~~why is it~~

why is it
That you live in the city?
where not everything
is all that pretty? and the only green grass
and crushed rock are being
well I look at them, smoked through a pipe
And after awhile
I begin to smile
because people live in the city
And people are my favorite Part of NATURE

Television

One nation
under god
has turned into
one nation under the influence
of one drug
television, the drug of the nation
breeding ignorance and feeding radiation

T.V., it
satellite links
our United States of unconsciousness
apathetic therapeutic and extremely addictive
the methadone metronome pumping out
150 channels 24 hours a day
you can flip through all of them
and still there's nothing worth watching

T.V. is the reason why less than ten percent of our
nation reads books daily
why most people think
Central America means Kansas
Socialism means unamerican
and Apartheid is a new headache remedy
absorbed in its world it's so hard to find us
it shapes our mind the most
maybe the mother of our nation
should remind us
that we're sitting to close to...

(chorus)
Television, the drug of the nation
breeding ignorance and feeding radiation

T.V. is
the stomping ground for political candidates
where bears in the woods
are chased by Grecian Formulad bald eagles
T.V. is mechanized politics
remote control over the masses
co-sponsored by environmentally safe gasses
watch for the PBS special
it's the perpetulation of the two party system
where image takes precedence over wisdom
where sound bite politics are served to
the fast food culture
where straight teeth in your mouth
are more important than the words
that come out of it
race baiting is the way to get selected
Willie Horton or will he not get elected on...

(chorus)

T.V. is it the reflector or the director?
does it imitate us
or do we imitate it
because a child watches 1500 murders before he's
twelve years old and we wonder how we've created
a Jason generation that learns to laugh
rather than abhor the horror
T.V. is the place where
armchair generals and quarterbacks can
experience first hand
the excitement of video warfare
as the theme song is sung in the background
sugar sweet sitcoms
that leave us with a bad after taste while
pop stars metamorphasize into soda pop stars
you saw the video
you heard the soundtrack
well now go buy the soft drink
well, the only cola that I support
would be a union C.O.L.A. (Cost Of
Living Allowance)
on television

(chorus)

Back again, "new and improved"
we return to our irregularly programmed schedule
hidden cleverly between heavily breasted
beer and car commercials
CNNESPNABCTNT but mostly B.S.
where oxymoronic language like
"virtually spotless" "fresh frozen"
"light yet filling" and "military intelligence"
have become standard
T.V. is the place where phrases are redefined
like "recession" to "necessary downturn"
"crude oil" on a beach to "mousse"
"civilian death" to "collateral damages"
and being killed by your own Army
is now called "friendly fire"
T.V. is the place where the pursuit of trivia
where toothpaste and cars have become sex objects
where imagination is sucked out of children
by a cathode ray nipple T.V. is
the only wet nurse
that would create a cripple

(chorus)

On television...

(previous page) Original draft of "Nature," 1986

Michael plays bass with The Beatnigs at the Ringold Alley Street Fair, 1987.
Photo by Eric Cope

CIA

CIA CIA CIA CIA Colonel North, Mr. Casey the CIA

Colonel North, Mr. Casey the CIA

diversion of funds covert arms sales in every country

the CIA mining harbors, Swiss bank accounts, hidden airstrips, cocaine sales

CIA CIA CIA CIA Colonel North, Mr. Casey the CIA

Colonel North, Mr. Casey the CIA

funding rebels with corporate interests fighting on every front

exciting arms secret hideaways the CIA the CIA

CIA CIA CIA CIA Colonel North, Mr. Casey the CIA

STREET FULLA NIGS

A street fulla people with fog in their heads
a street fulla people in chains
a street fulla people when
the lights come on tomorrow won't change
a street fulla transfers attached to waving arms
a street fulla dirty drivers in shiny cars
my street's fulla dollars
hold as tight as wrinkles in their hands

A street fulla nigs in nylon leather jackets
a street fulla blacks who are chained
a street fulla TV's shouting morals in their ears
a street fulla complainers in Macy's suits
a street fulla faceless names
a street fulla privileged sufferers
settling for Italian motorcycles

And it might lead to a life in the White House
or it might lead to a wife and a white house I don't know
but the day I die the day I die
it'll be a normal day for the people on the other side
a street fulla nigs

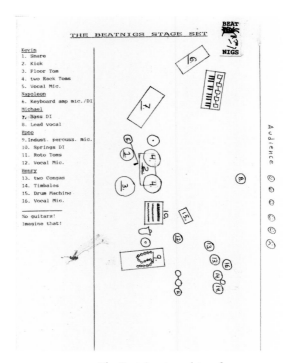

The Beatnigs stage plot, 1987

CONTROL

Control! in South Africa today military sources reported that
the rioting in the homeland has increased
the system of apartheid is slipping
in South Africa today military sources reported that
four miners were killed and twenty one injured in racially motivated violence
in South Africa today military sources reported that
a peaceful compromise could not be reached
what sort of peaceful compromise could be reached after years of violence?
in South Africa today military sources were sad to say
that the system of apartheid is finished!
but we must maintain control
we must maintain control
we must maintain control
freedom freedom free yourself freedom
freedom freedom free yourself,
freedom

*Michael rocks the bass and Kevin Carnes
beats the drums in the background, while Rono
Tse takes the angle grinder to a gas tank.
At The Farm in San Francisco, 1987. Photo by Eric Cope*

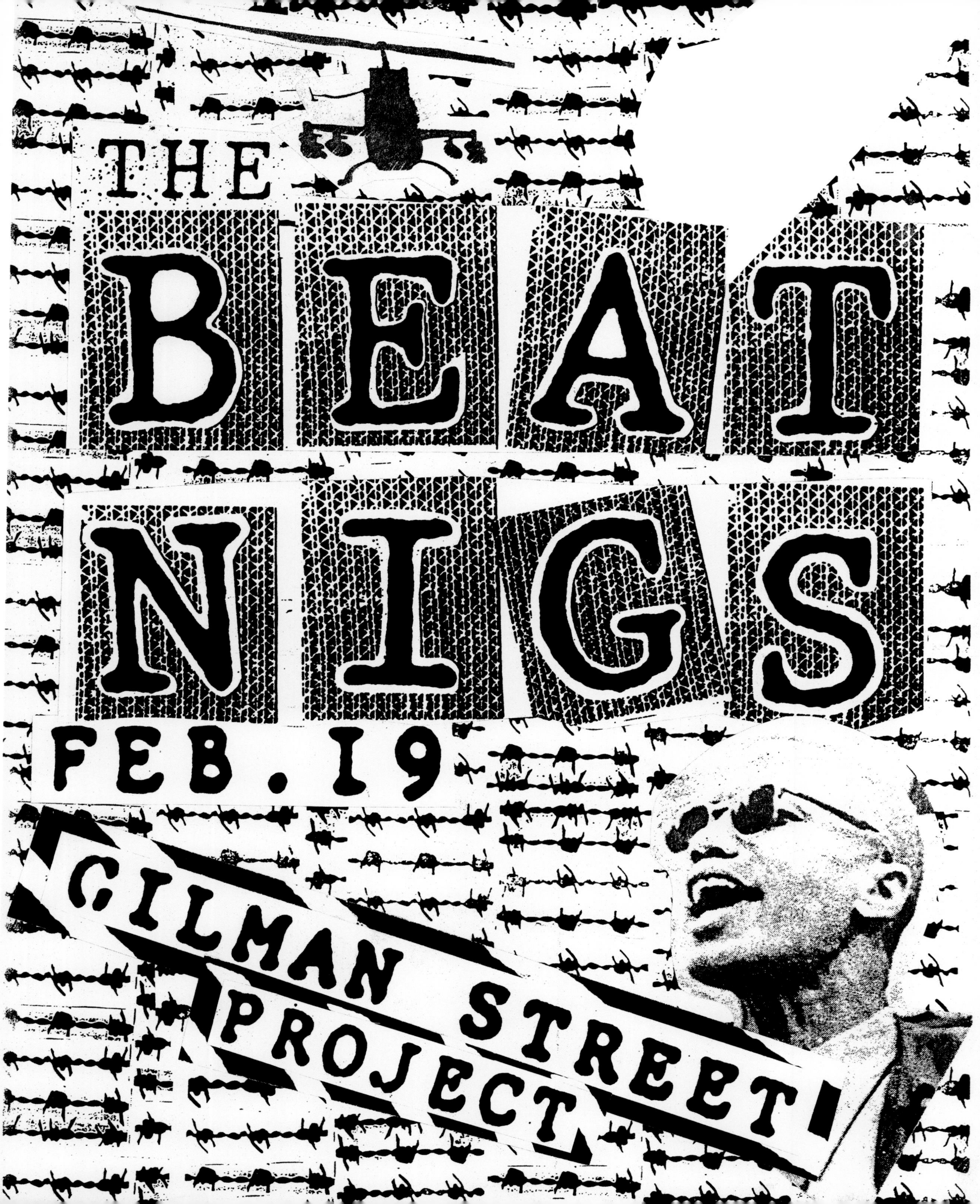
THE
BEAT
NIGS
FEB. 19
GILMAN STREET
PROJECT

MALCOLM X

It's incredible that one man could build up such momentum
that in his death his inertia spawned a generation
it was plain for them to see what he meant to you and me
one to the chin and one to the chest couldn't stop the movement
and his name is Malcolm X
here in this holy place we come to bear witness
to a man who means so much to us
to those of you who never knew Malcolm X
you may consider him a militant, a radical, a terrorist
but to those of you who ever heard him speak or
ever once read anything that he wrote, or ever held his hand
you would know him for what he truly was
a prince, our own shining prince
who gave his life because he loved us so

NATURE

Nature
sitting in the green grass
watching the strange world of ants

Nature
at the beach watching rocks smash into pebbles
and whisper into sand
people often ask me,
"Michael if you love nature so much
why is it that you live in the city
where the only green grass and crushed rock
is being smoked through a pipe?"
well I look at them and tell 'em
"Cause people live in the city
and people are the best part of nature"
so the next time you go to a shecky club
put on your shecky hairspray, put on your shecky make-up,
remember that people still eat, people still think and people still defecate!
no matter how hard we try to dehumanize, and dehumanize,
with ID numbers, credit card numbers, Social Security numbers

People are the best part of nature
people are the best part of nature
people are the best part of nature

*Flyer for one of The Beatnigs' many shows
at the legendary punk rock club The Gilman
Street Project, Berkeley, California, 1987*

Flyer from Beatnigs show, 1986

HYPOCRISY IS THE GREATEST LUXURY

1991

If I could ever stop thinking...

If I could ever stop thinking
about music and politics

I would tell you that sometimes it's easier
to desire and pursue the attention and admiration
of one hundred strangers than it is
to accept the love and loyalty of those closest
to me.

and I would tell you the easier way is usually
what I choose.

I would tell you that sometimes I prefer
to look at myself through someone's eyes
that are not clouded with the ~~tears~~ of
knowing ~~how careless~~ what an asshole I can be.
as yours are.

If I could ever stop thinking about music
and politics

Change
I might be able to listen...in silence...to ~~all~~
~~your~~ your concerns/ rather than hear everything
as an accusation or indictment against me.

I would tell you that sometimes I use
sex to avoid communications.
and that I can actually express more emotions
than laughter, anger, and "let's fuck".

I would tell you that I pooped in
my own dog dish and that I would

(previous page) Original draft of Disposable Heroes of Hiphoprisy song "Music and Politics," 1990.

Bono and Michael flashing peace on U2's jet,
1992 Photo by anonymous

SATANIC REVERSES

In the 1970's
the POPEC nations began to dominate
the world's oil economy
in the 1980's Japan became the world's
number ONE economic power
in 1989 the nations of Eastern Europe
attempted to restructure
while in the United States civil rights have
collapsed at the hands of fundamentalists
and national security's at an all time high

Exxon and on and on and on
the ministers of double speak
new meaning of clean they
tried to teach us
they staged the phony shampoo of the
Valdez greases
completely jheri curled the beaches
pipe bomb for the NAACP
and a hit on Salman Rushdie
the Berlin Wall comes down and the U.S. cracks down
on illegal aliens
ban the freedom of choice for those
wanting abortion
and enforce capitol punishment
twenty four hour radio ban
for indecency determined by the F.U.C.C.
why are we so anesthetized to the lies
because we do it in our own lives
we believe all the things that we want to hear
but then love to criticize

Bail-out the banks loan art to the churches
Satanic Reverses

In 1992 the European economic community will reform
in 1997 the city of Hong Kong will become a part
of the People's Republic of China
in 1999, and this is no coincidence,
the nation of Panama will control it's own canal
while in the United States civil rights have
collapsed at the hands of fundamentalists
and the national insecurity's at an all time high

Helms said ban the photograph
of the piss Christ
it's sacreligious not an art piece

While we all try to discern between
our cup of tea and what we call obscenity the house's legislation
ripped the phony foundation
off what we thought inherent
sent Joey to the Supreme Court

Cause he made a statement
they called it desecration
of the symbol that was meant to represent
the freedom of so called choice and dissent
they almost had me believing it
they were bleeding him
he said, "burn baby, burn"
'Til the street samurai
said to my face that
any flag that's worth a shit
was woven from fire in the first place.

Bail-out the banks loan art to the churches
Satanic Reverses

Michael in dugout at Yankee stadium before
opening for U2 on the ZooTV tour, 1992
Photo by Ras-I-Zulu

FAMOUS AND DANDY (LIKE AMOS AND ANDY)

(chorus)
What will we do to become famous and dandy,
just like Amos 'n' Andy
what will we do to become famous 'n' dandy,
just like Amos 'n' Andy

It's quite a spectacle to see us land in
waste receptacles as if we've planned it
we're never skeptical when we get branded
then disrespectful 'Cause we feel abandoned
the height of mediocrity is the challenge
crawling through the entrails of imbalance
we learn to like to be the heroes
we learn to lie to be brand name negroes
we learn to laugh to avoid being angry
we learn to kill and learn to go hungry
we learn not to feel, for protection
and we learn to flaunt when we get an erection

(chorus)

We're born believing we're greater than circumstance
infinitely stronger than chance
as our first breath is handed we taste the double standard

The need to wear the mask and with society's nurturing
the psychic plastic surgery
begins to take effect
as our souls watch astounded our characters flounder
duplicitous identity
diction and contradiction have become the skills of assimilation
razor honed to perfection from the moment of creation
it's gone from identity crisis to survival
slingshot to rifle
sin to revival
try to get looked at but not poked in the eyeball
warned of our impurities afraid of insecurities
real life experts of the artificial
athletes and entertainers
have become the minstrels on commercials

(chorus)

On screen or off we can be rented
to perform any feat
and we reflect the images presented
by the media's elite
positive or negative attention is viewed as success
U.S.D.A. African American Beef is seen as progress
we never ask ourselves too many questions
too much truth in introspection
maintain the regimentation
and avoid self-degradation we act out all the stereotypes
try to use them as decoy
and we become shining examples
of the system we set out to destroy
'cause even in the most radical of groups
you will find that when you stray from the doctrine
you'll see hard times

(chorus)

Being kicked in the closed mouth
or smiling with no teeth
they're both choices, yes
but it's impossible to eat
uneducated underdeveloped
undisciplined but mostly unaware
we join the flavor of the month club
we swallow their flavor of the month
holding our crotch was the flavor of the month
bitch this bitch that was the flavor of the month
being a thug was the flavor of the month
no to drugs was the flavor of the month
Kangol was the flavor of the month
rope gold was the flavor of the month
Adiddas shoes was the flavor of the month
bashing Jews was the flavor of the month
gentrification was the flavor of the month
isolation was the flavor of the month
my pockets so empty I can feel my testicles
'Cause I spent all my money
on some plastic African necklaces
and I still don't know what the colors mean...
red, black and green

(chorus)

Michael, Self Portrait, San Francisco 1992

TELEVISION,
THE DRUG OF THE NATION

One nation
under god
has turned into
one nation under the influence
of one drug
television, the drug of the nation
breeding ignorance and feeding radiation

T.V., it
satellite links
our United States of unconsciousness
apathetic therapeutic and extremely addictive
the methadone metronome pumping out
150 channels 24 hours a day
you can flip through all of them
and still there's nothing worth watching
T.V. is the reason why less than ten percent of our
nation reads books daily
why most people think Central America means Kansas
Socialism means unamerican

*Bono, William S. Burroughs, James Grauerholz,
Hal Wilner, Rono Tse, and Michael in the emer-
gency exit stairs of the Four Seasons hotel in
Kansas City, 1992. Posing with a few of Mr.
Burroughs's handguns. Photos by Vaughn
Martinian*

and Apartheid is a new headache remedy
absorbed in it's world it's so hard to find us
it shapes our mind the most
maybe the mother of our nation
should remind us
that we're sitting to close to...

    (chorus)
Television, the drug of the nation
breeding ignorance and feeding radiation

T.V. is
the stomping ground for political candidates
where bears in the woods
are chased by Grecian Formulad bald eagles
T.V. is mechanized politics
remote control over the masses

co-sponsored by environmentally safe gasses
watch for the PBS special
it's the perpetulation of the two party system
where image takes precedence over wisdom
where sound bite politics are served to
the fast food culture
where straight teeth in your mouth
are more important than the words
that come out of it
race baiting is the way to get selected
Willie Horton or
will he not get elected on...

(chorus)

T.V. is it the reflector or the director?
does it imitate us
one nation
under god
has turned into

one nation under the influence of one drug

(chorus)

T.V. is it the reflector or the director?
does it imitate us
or do we imitate it
because a child watches 1500 murders before he's
twelve years old and we wonder how we've created
a Jason generation that learns to laugh
rather than abhor the horror
T.V. is the place where
armchair generals and quarterbacks can
experience first hand
the excitement of video warfare
as the theme song is sung in the background

sugar sweet sitcoms
that leave us with a bad aafter taste while
pop stars metamorphasize into soda pop stars
you saw the video
you heard the soundtrack
well now go buy the soft drink
well, the only cola that I support
would be a union C.O.L.A. (Cost Of Living Allowance)
on television

(chorus)

Back again, "new and improved"
we return to our irregularlly programmed schedule
hidden cleverly between heavily breasted
beer and car commercials
CNNESPNABCTNT but mostly B.S.
where oxymoronic language like
"virtually spotless" "fresh frozen"
"light yet filling" and "military intelligence"

have become standard
T.V. is the place where phrases are redefined
like "recession" to "necessary downturn"
"crude oil" on a beach to "mousse"
"civilian death" to "collateral damages"
and being killed by your own Army
is now called "friendly fire"
T.V. is the place where the pursuit of trivia
where toothpaste and cars have become sex objects
where imagination is sucked out of children
by a cathode ray nipple T.V. is
the only wet nurse
that would create a cripple

(chorus)

On television...

*Michael and Rono at the at a drag ball
in Montreal on the ZooTV tour. 1992
Photos by Vaughn Martinian*

LANGUAGE OF VIOLENCE

The first day of school was always the hardest
the first day of school the hallways the darkest

Like a gauntlet
the voices haunted
walking in with his thin skin
lowered chin
he know the names they would taunt him with
faggot, sissy. punk, queen, queer
although he'd never had sex in his fifteen years
and when they harassed him
it was for a reason
and when they provoked him
it became open season
for the fox and the hunter

the sparks and the thunder
that pushed the boy under
then pillage and plunder
it kind of makes me wonder
how one can hurt another

But dehumanizing the victim makes things simpler
it's like breathing with a respirator
it eases the consciousness of even the most conscious
and calculating violator
words can reduce a person to an object
something more easy to hate
an inanimate entity
completely disposable
no problem to obliterate

But death is the silence
in this language of violence
death is the silence
but death is the silence
in this cycle of violence
death is the silence

It's tough to be young
the young long to be tougher
when we pick on someone else
it might make us feel rougher
abused by our fathers
but that was at home though
so to prove to each other
that they were not "homos"
the exclamation of the phobic fury
executioner, judge and jury
the mob mentality
individuality was nowhere
dignity forgotten
at the bottom of a dumb old dare
and a numb cold stare
on the way home it was back to name calling
ten against one they had his back up against the wall and
they reveled in their laughter
as they surrounded him
but it wasn't a game
when they up jumped and grounded him
they picked up their bats
with their muscles strainin'
and they decided they were gonna
beat this fella's brain in
with an awful powerful
showerful an hour full of violence
inflict the strictest
brutality and dominance
they didn't hear him screaming
they didn't hear him pleading
they ran like cowards
and left the boy bleeding
in a pool of red
'til all tears were shed
and his eyes quietly slid
into the back of his head
DEAD...

    (chorus)
You won't see the face 'til the eyelids drop
you won't hear the screaming until it stops

The boy's parents were gone

and his grandmother had raised him
she was mad she had no form
of retaliation
the pack didn't have to worry about
being on a hit list
but the thing they never thought about
was that there was a witness
to this senseless crime
right place wrong time
tried as an adult
one of them was gonna do hard time

The first day of prison was always the hardest
the first day of prison the hallways the darkest

Like a gauntlet
the voices haunted
faggot, sissy. punk, queen, queer
words he used before had a new meaning in here
as a group of men in front of him laughing came near
for the first time in his life
the young bully felt fear
he'd never been on this side of the name calling
five against one they had his back up against the wall and
he had never questioned his own sexuality
but this group of men didn't hesitate their reality
with an awful powerful
showerful an hour full of violence
inflict the strictest
brutality and dominance
they didn't hear him screaming
they didn't hear him pleading
they took what they wanted
and then just left him bleeding in the corner
the giant reduced to Jack Horner

But dehumanizing the victim makes things simpler
it's like breathing with a respirator
it eases the consciousness of even the most conscious
and calculating violator
the power of words
don't take it for granted
when you hear a man ranting
don't just read the lips
be more sublime than this
put everything in context
is this a tale of rough justice
in a land where there's no justice at all
who is really the victim?
or are we all the cause and victim of it all

    (chorus)

WINTER OF THE LONG HOT SUMMER

It all seemed so idiotic all the accusations of unpatriotic
the fall we'll always remember capitulating silence
election November before the winter
of the long hot summer
somewhere in the desert
we raised the oil pressure
and waited for the weather to get much better
for the new wind to blow in the storm
we tried to remember the history of the region
the French foreign legion, Imperialism
Peter O'Toole and hate the Ayatollah
were all we learned in school
not that we gave Hussein five billion
not of our new bed partner the Syrian
and of course no mention of the Palestinian situation
it was amazing how they steamrolled
they said eighty percent approval
but there was no one that I knew polled
no one had a reason for being in the Gulf
we waited for congress to speak up illegal build up
but no one would wake up

Our representatives were Milli Vanilli's
for corporate Dallas Cowboy Beverly Hillbillies
with perfect timing
the politicians rhyming their sentiments
so nicely oil gold and sand
my sediments precisely...
we regretfully support the lunacy
I'm afraid there is no time for more scrutiny
National unity preserve our community
Teflon® election opportunities
were in profundant abundance

On January second the Bush administration
announced a recession had stricken
the Nation the highest quarterly
earnings in ten years were posted
by Chevron®
meanwhile a budget was placed in our hands
as the deadline in the sand came to an end
so much for the peace dividend
one billion a day is what we spent
and our grandchildren will pay for it 'til the end
when schools are unfunded
and kids don't get their diplomas

they get used for for gunboat diplomacy
disproportionately
black or brown we see
bullet catchers for the slave master

Then the conservatives called up reservists
to active service left families nervous
but more importantly broke nine hundred a month
but the check came late you see,army red tape you see
this golden opportunity
we watched the tube and read the newspaper
the propaganda of the gas masked rapper
was the proper slander to whip up the hatred

The stage was lit and the lights were all faded
the pilots in night vision goggles Kuwaited and
generals masturbated
'til the fifteenth two days later they invaded
not a single t.v. station expressed dissension or
hardly made mention to the censorship of information
from our kinder and gentler nation
blinder and mentaler retardation
DISORIENTATION

The pilots said their bombs lit Baghdad
like a Christmas tree
it was the Christian thing to do you see
they didn't mention any casualties
no distinction between the real
and the proxy
only football analogies
we saw the bomb hole
we watched the Super Bowl
we saw the scud missile
we watched the Bud® commercials
we saw the yellow ribbons
we saw pilots in prison
we never saw films of the dead...at eleven
Angela Davis addressed the spectators
and shouting above a rumbling generator said
if they insist on bringing this down
then let's shut the whole country down
marching through the downtown
a hundred thousand became participants
and we heard the drums of millions off in the distance
rushing through the streets

Michael, San Francisco 1987. Photo Andre Flores

some of them did things that weren't so pretty
most were there for primal scream therapy
news men concentrated
on the negitive liked the jingoists more
peaceful protesters ended up
on the cutting room floor
Nintendo® casualties of the ratings war
more bombs dropped than in World War II
or in both Asian invasions, new world order persuasion,
business as usual for our nation
could you imagine a hundred and fifty thousand dead,
the city of Stockton
coffins locked in when we clocked in...
not to mention civilians
the loss of life on both sides
pushed the limits of resilience
the scent of blood in our nostrils
fuel of the fossil land of apostle
the blackness that covered the sky was not the only thing

that brought a tear to the eye or
the taste of anger to the tongues
of those too young to remember Vietnam
Is heroin better in a veteran's mind
than the memory of the dying lying in a line
is it the smell or the shadows heaving and weeping
that keeps the soldier from sleeping
as he sings the orphan's lullaby
when the soldiers put down their bayonets
the strings are chained to the marionettes
Emir of Kuwait gets back in his jet
we replace the dead with new cadets
will we hate those that did the shelling
or will we hate those who weren't willing to do the killing
when the leaders of the bald eagles come home to roost
will we sing a song of praise and indebtedness
for our deliverance from evil
or will we sing a song of sadness
for the dreaded debt this mess delivered us PEOPLE

Hypocrisy Is The Greatest Luxury

Life these days
can be so complex
we don't make the time
to stop and reflect
I know from first hand experience
one can go delirious
seriously it can be like that
but before I put my foot in my mouth
'cause that's what I'm about
to start talkin' about
please let me confess before all the rest
that I'm afflicted
by this addicted like most in the U.S.
it's tough to make a living when you're an artist
it's even tougher when you're socially conscious
careerism, opportunism
can turn the politics into cartoonism
let's not patronize or criticize
let's open the door and look inside
put the file on this state of denial

Hypocrisy is the greatest luxury
raise the double standard

Life these days
can be so complex
we don't make the time
to stop and reflect
I know from first hand experience
one can go delirious
seriously it can be like that
but before I put my foot in my mouth
'cause that's what I'm about
to start talkin' about
please let me confess before all the rest
that I'm afflicted
by this addicted like most in the U.S.
it's tough to make a living when you're an artist
it's even tougher when you're socially conscious
careerism, opportunism
can turn the politics into cartoonism
let's not patronize or criticize
let's open the door and look inside
put the file on this state of denial

Hypocrisy is the greatest luxury
raise the double standard

Michael backstage at Foxboro Stadium
Massachusetts, 1992
Photo by Ras-I-Zulu

Everyday Life Has Become a Health Risk

The wind shifted
back in the fifties particles drifted
a wave set in motion
the Pacific Ocean
test of the hydrogen bomb
there from would come
too close to home
ships from the test
put to rest
and convalesce with heavily armed guard
in Hunter's Point shipyard
heavy metal sandblast
facemask
deoxidize
remove the radiation from the outside
a hazardous cargo
dumped into the harbor
went farther than that though
sand from the blasting
made into sidewalks
played on by kids who just got over chicken-pox
glowing faces
all races
hop-scotch bare feet
on Geiger counter concrete
mother prepares a fruit salad treat to eat
sprayed with messed up pesticides
none have been tested for health effects
on the side

     (chorus)
Medical racist, social statistics
has everyday life become a health risk
Medical racist, social statistics
has everyday life become a health risk

Meanwhile, back in the backyard,
father lights up a barbeque fire
and he sizzles hormone injected meat
on top of a toxic source of heat
he becomes light headed
as the toxins easily meet
with the light beer in his head and
he glances to his portable television set
from his eyes he wipes the double vision sweat
visions of white supremacists
posing as right conservationists
holding an Aryan agrarian Woodstock
lead the stray sheep into the flock
hookin' 'em in with the music of flower power
change their energy into fire power

     (chorus)

All of a sudden
acid rain falls from the sky
and gets into the nuclear family picnic pie
not to mention the Kool Aid®
the nuclear family sits down to lunch
they munch it down with acid rain punch
and they begin to hallucinate
disassociate the pain in their bodies
from the pain in their minds
they go inside and remember a time
before the world went
completely blind
when people grew bald naturally
no mutations
unlike Skinheads
and kemo-therapy patients

     (chorus)

SOCIO-GENETIC EXPERIMENT

Sometimes I feel like a socio-genetic experiment
a petri-dish community's token of infection

You see I'm African, Native American
Irish and German
I was adopted by parents who loved me
they were the same color
as the kids who called me nigger
on the walk home from school
I cried until I found out what it meant
then I got me some equipment
my fists, man
I was a hitman with no friends
but who the hell am I cursing those
whose skin is half my DNA
why am I
and why shouldn't I
be ashamed of this fact
after all the feces they dumped
on me and my species

(chorus)

Those mother...
shut 'cho mouth
there I go again with those high and mighty speeches
when they are in fact part of my species
or is it the other way around
did I piss in their gene pool
if I did it wouldn't matter
they kept me in the deep end

'cause the dilution
in their solution
was perceived as pollution

(chorus)

But I am not solely race, nor environment, nor destiny
I am the human scientific process
over and over and over again
the dirt that I shovel to uncover the truth
often buries something else growing
acceptance of my own weakness
and my own intolerance is seldom
but that is in fact my identity
uncluttered by the maskings of consumer addiction
ethno-centricity
in the light of miscegenation
this fable of elements
which classify order species, sub-species
genus phyla
animal vegetable illegal chemical
socialist democrat republican
yuppy-buppy-guppy
proud racist
black, white, African, Native American, Irish and German

(chorus)

And I'm proud

Early draft of "Socio-Genetic Experiment," 1990

A poem about my constant struggle to
come to grips with my own multiethnicity
in a racist society and my own racial biases
which have come as a result of it.

Sometimes I Feel Like a
Socio-Genetic Experiment

The taboo of multiethnicity

MUSIC AND POLITICS

If ever I would stop thinking about music and politics
I would tell you that sometimes
it's easier to desire and pursue the attention and
admiration of a hundred strangers
than it is to accept the love and loyalty
of those closest to me.

And I would tell you that sometimes
I prefer to look at myself through someone else's eyes
eyes that aren't clouded with the tears of knowing
what an asshole I can be, as yours are

If ever I would stop thinking about music and politics
I might be able to listen in silence to your concerns
rather than hearing everything as an accusation or an
indictment
against me

And I would tell you that sometimes
I use sex to avoid communication
It's the best escape when we're down on our luck
but I can express more emotions
than laughter, anger and "let's fuck"

If ever I would stop thinking about music and politics
If ever I would stop thinking about music and politics
If ever I would stop thinking about music and politics
If ever I would stop thinking about music and politics

If ever I would stop thinking about music and politics
I would tell you that I pooped in my own dog dish
and sometimes I would rather face not eating
than face licking it clean
and admitting when I'm selfish
and I'd tell you that I'm suffering from the worst type of loneliness
the loneliness of being misunderstood
or more poignantly
the loneliness of being afraid to allow myself
to be understood

If ever I would stop thinking about music and politics
I would tell you that the personal revolution
is far more difficult
and the first step
in any revolution

If ever I would stop thinking about music and politics
If ever I would stop thinking about music and politics
If ever I would stop thinking about music and politics
If ever I would stop thinking about music and politics

I would tell you that music is the expression of emotion
and that politics is merely the decoy of perception

FINANCIAL LEPROSY

Financial leprosy
we got to get up and wait in line
for the soup, toilets and things to read
fill out 11-0-1s and take a seat
but then we got to find a place to sleep
we got to lay down upon newspaper, cardboard, concrete
and plastic sheets
effects of eighties' public policy
we used to buy full shopping carts and buy useless products
trained to drain, not to remain
red-line economy
"I have a dream"'s reality

Well, self-effacing and mirror-hating
the ethnic potions and lotions
but I still smell bad
skin fader and tanning booths
in conjunction with their plastic boobs and diet pills

    (chorus)
All means to attract and distract
All means to attract and distract
All means to attract and distract
All means to attract and distract

Designer glasses to see designer clothes
designer cologne to wave under a designer drug nose
that sniffs through the perfume-scented magazines
try to make sense out of dollars
often heard of, rarely seen
as an ear listens to the dial tone
I pretend to talk on a cellular phone
that I know I can't afford

well, I used to own this street
and now I'm living on Market Street

    (chorus)

Thieves generating revenues
lottery poverty tax
druglords and landlords and "praise the lords"
they prey upon us
how did they ever manufacture consent?
a meal in every trashcan
myth of "the happy hobo"
COINTELPRO (COunter INTELligence PROgram)
"The Cosby Show"
why did they cut the Pell Grant?
so they can build cells
ten years in prison but no tenure at the university
Is this ethnic diversity?
Or is it public policy?

    (chorus)

Chemical bullets
aimed at the Afro Diaspora
a genocidal ghost manipulates
a suicidal host
and as high technology
eliminates the need for manual labor
and Mercedes Benz logos replace peace signs
on the necks of our youth

    (chorus)

Rono Tse, Michael and Iggy Pop at the Big Day Out Festival. Adelaide, Australia, 1991

WATER PISTOL MAN

When girls dressed in black they all look so lonely
and contraceptives don't get used by the horny
you can't find the key to the door in your building
but you are still willing
the responsibility becomes an afterthought
when one remembers the things that they should've bought
there's no pretending that you forgot
must everything in life have political ramifications
even taking kids on vacation or having a simple operation
but my friend Billy told me that sometimes it takes a grown man
a long time to learn just what it takes a child a night to learn
and my son proved his words

    (chorus)
Water pistol man full of ammunition
squirtin' at fires on a worldwide mission
but did you ever think to stop to squirt the flowers
in your own backyard

For all my faux pas I never said excuse me
was the simplest things that always confused me
I never stopped I never looked both ways
must it always be a tug of love between friends and work
hope to learn the meaning of the word jerk
before it happens to a rope 'round my neck
let's build a bigger telescope
so that we can see things more up close
farther away from where we really are
I was up the whole night before
reading books about places I'll probably never go
and those aren't good things to know about

    (chorus)

When I feel with my heart, I know in my mind
I should say with my lips, but don't
does that make you feel upset? I should know that
the power of one man seems like a smart squirt
when he aims at the flames of the whole earth
but the fire starts at home...

    (chorus)

Michael loading in at Leoncovello, Milan, Italy, 2001

HOME
1994

⑤ And what I see ~~when I look in your~~
When I look in your eyes
Is a grass that's truly greenest
~~In your inside~~ ~~Is your~~ sprouting ~~boom~~ inside

⑥ I wasn't even lookin'
When I realized
That you had the vibe
That ~~is~~ was my fertilizer

⑦ You hit me in the chest
like an 808 Boom!
~~because~~ I found Love is the SHIT
that makes life bloom

⑧ Yes love is the shit that makes life Bloom
and I ~~may~~ never know when I ~~come~~ might step in it

⑨ But fate is like a pigeon
that follows me around
~~He~~ Sometimes he flies ~~a~~ ahead
and brings me what he found
Then he'll drop it on my head
~~and~~ leave numb from the brain down ↓
That's ~~the way~~ the way it was
When ~~I came to your town~~ I walked upon your ground.

⑩ The irrepressable
and imermissable
are the two things
that've made my life miserable

PEOPLE IN THA MIDDLE

I am not a Muslim but I read the final call
because within its pages there is something for us all
and I am not professional, but I love basketball
the squeakin' of the sneakers they echo in the hall
but if I don't have enemies I'm not doin' my job
I might throw out a curve ball but I never throw a lob
people criticize me but I know it's not the end
I try to kick the truth not just to make friends

> *(chorus)*
> *But hey diddle diddle*
> *to the people in the middle*
> *we got hot wax*
> *and it's cookin' on the griddle*
> *got the guitar strummin'*
> *the drummer drummin'*
> *the people all hummin'*
> *and the vibe was lovin'*
> *on and on and on*
> *'till the breakadawn*

I am not a jerk although sometimes I act like one
and I am deadly serious about us havin' fun
well I go many places but I know I'm not with you
and I am not a sucka even though I'm stuck on you
each one should teach one and share with one anotha
so many is out there—that's livin' undercover
your motha your fatha your sista your brotha
your friends and their enemies all have their lovers yeah!

> *(chorus)*

So tell me the definition of a "sell out"
cast your first stone—but then you get the hell out
people say they know me I can tell you that they don't
people say they own me I can tell you that they won't
the left and the right they all try to use me
but I'll be in they faces before they can abuse me
so roll down ya window and listen what I'm sayin'
relax ya mind let the band keep playin'
on and on and on 'till the breakadawn

> *(chorus)*

Michael, exuberant on stage, Milan, Italy, 2001

(previous page) Original draft of the song "Love Is Da Shit," San Francisco, 1993

Arriving in Rotterdam, Holland for Dunya Fest, 2001

LOVE IS DA SHIT

Say when you called me that night
to tell me that things
they weren't goin' alright with your boyfriend
was it me or did you just want someone to talk to
say is it you or the fact that I can't be near you
that keeps you in the front of my mind
when your voice goes away
and a breath is the last thing that you say

But the warmth of your lips on my fingertips
won't go away
when I drop my head in my hands and play
the memory of that night in L.A.
again and again and again
because I can't think straight and I can't sleep late
the few times we shared I try to recreate
I know this is wrong better stop this talk
because grass can grow up through a crack in the sidewalk
and what I see when I look in your eyes
grass that's truly greenest sprouting inside
I wasn't even looking when I realized
that you had the vibe that was my fertilizer
thought love in this world was dead and buried and gone
how could I be so cynical when I was so young
you hit me in the chest like an 808 boom
I found love is the shit that makes life bloom!

   (chorus)
   Love is the shit that makes life bloom
   and you never know when you might step in it!
   love is the shit that makes life bloom
   and you never know when you might...

But fate is like a pigeon that follows me around
sometimes he flies ahead and he brings me what he found
then he'll drop it on my head leave me numb from the brain down
that's the way it was when I walked upon your ground

the irrepressible and impermissible
are the two things that have made my life miserable
'cause spirits don't leave if you don't talk about 'em
and memories come back when you don't think about 'em

I wish I had an ocean of some magic potion
I'd trade all this emotion for a few moments of motion
I've never felt this way some things can't be rehearsed
now I'm grindin' up my gearbox tryin' to find reverse
because...

   (chorus)

   (bridge)
But I want to keep on walking
right through
and let this feeling rock me
ooh-oooh!

   (chorus)

Ya know fallin' in love is like easing into a hot tub
it feels good on your feet but by the time you
get to your midsection you know you're either
gonna get all the way in or all the way out!

But music brings me comfort in this grieving hour
the Sade tape tells me it's all over for now
I listen real hard but don't dare play it loud
'cause I don't wanna think what you might be doin' now
sometimes it feels like a bad initiation but you
woke my heart from a long hibernation
you were worth every risk so I gave my heart room
and now I'm deep in the doo-doo
that makes life bloom
because...

   (chorus)

   (bridge)
See the flowers bloom' in the springtime
see the bees zoomin' in the sunshine
   (repeat)

PIECE O' PEACE

Every million mile ya haffe tek a first step
Every million mile ya haffe tek a first step

I was sick of flippin channels and sick of flippin' quarters
I called my man Zulu said, "Meet me on the corner."
maybe we can check out the clubs in the city
'cause waitin at the crib can make you feel shitty
so he hopped into my ride on the squeaky door side
and we hit the Upper Room where they keep the funk alive
the man at the door invited us inside
he said there isn't any cover if you're keepin' up the vibe

We took it up stairs to big up the area
the people in the house was shakin' up their derriere
raisin up their hands and raisin up their voices
Tokes was the D.J. I was happy with his choices
maxin' and mixin' tha beats they was fixin'
my brain like a smoke that was doubly, triply, dope
the decadence is gone and life may never be the same
'cause when the beat hits you feel no pain!

(chorus)
So a piece of peace for you, a piece of peace for me
a piece of peace for every peaceful person that you see
a piece of peace for you and a piece of peace for me
but I don't act peaceful if you're not that way to me
every million mile ya haffe tek a first step
every million mile ya haffe tek a first step

Five-O was outside waitin' with their vans
hopin' that shit would get outta hand
so dat they could test their weapons on innocent civilians,
the high tech shit costin' millions and millions
money should've spent on somethin' for community
but that's O.K. 'cause we got the unity
so fuck the police! we can keep the peace!
we can make love and conquer that disease
'case nuttin in the world is impossible to me
I can swim on dry land and run upon the sea
and nuttin in the world is impossible to me
you can chop off my legs and I'll land upon my feet
I turn it over to the spirit and I leave her in charge

my favorite record sounds like an African Head Charge
she'll beat up the beats with an eggbeater
pour em in the batter
she'll make 'em sound fatter and fatter
'cause food for the soul is the flavor of the music
spice for the brain is the essence of the lyrics
songs can be delicious and also be nutritious
You can't pay for culture, it can only be experienced
BOOM! BOOM! BOOM!
"WELL HAVE YOU EVER BEEN EXPERIENCED!"
"WELL"
every million mile ya haffe tek a step
every million mile ya haffe tek a step

(chorus)

If the funk is on time
then we call it punctual
we're matchin up the footsteps
spiritual and functional
like Carnivale in Rio
the Charlie Hunter trio
had the groovers groovvin'
and all the movers movin'
Cuba, Twist, Reminisce, and NME
graffiti on the street for everyone to see
even the elders in the house was havin' fun
because we livin' life at the top of our lungs
it was truly a life celebration that night
had the world's greatest time
but we'd never sell the movie rights
to Maury Povich, or anyone like that
and anyone who does is really, really whack!
we fish or cut bait and we're not takin' prisoners and
if you comin' late then you might've missed some a this
funky good time we had here in fronta you
so long, farewell, alveedersain, adieau to you

(chorus)

Every million mile ya haffe tek a first step
every million mile ya haffe tek a first step

Michael at the Sugar Shack, San Francisco, 2002

Michael doing a little 3:30 am yoga outside The Palookaville Club. Santa Cruz, California, 2000

POSITIVE

Make me, make me sweat
till I'm wet, till I'm dry
but then wipe this tear from my eye
haven't felt this warm in a long time
even out in the bright sunshine
in a lifetime of springtimes

I fall into your arms
with my heart pumpin' on
like a bubblin' dub track
like a garlicy hot tongue and lip smack

I did some contemplation
before we got down to this consecration
maybe baby something in your kiss said
it was an impetus for me to re-think think

If I love you, then I better get tested
make sure we're protected
I walk through the park
dressed like a question mark
hark!
I hear my memory bark
in the back of my brain,
makin' me insane...
...like cocaine

(chorus)
But how'm I gonna live my life if I'm positive?
is it gonna be a negative?
how'm I gonna live my life if I'm positive?
is it gonna be a negative?
but how'm I gonna live my life if I'm positive?

It dawned on me, it seemed to me
this is unusual scenery,
this red light greenery
make me feel kinda dreamery,
thinkin' how I used to be

Arrive at the clinic
walk through the front door
take a nervous number

then I think some more
about all the time that I neglected
makin sure that I was protected

They took my blood
with an anonymous number
two weeks waitin' wonderin'

I shoulda done this a long time ago
a lot of excuses why I couldn't go
I know these things and these things I must know
'cause it's better to know than not to know!

(chorus)

I go home to kick it in my apartment
I try to give myself a risk assessment
the wait is what can really annoy ya
everyday's more paronoya

I'm readin' about how it's transmitted
some behavior I must admit it
who I slept with, who they slept with,
who they, who they, who they slept with

I think about life and immortality
what's the first thing I do if I'm H.I.V.
have a cry and tell my mother
get on the phone and call my past lovers
I never thought about infectin' anotha
all the times that I said "Hmm? Don't bother."

Was it really all that magic?
the times I didn't use a prophylactic

would my whole life have to change?
or would my whole life remain the same?
sometimes it makes me wanna shout!
all these things too hard to think about
a day to laugh, a day to cry
a day to live and a day to die
'till I found out, I may wonder
but I'm not gonna live my life six feet under

Michael on the 'Growing Up W/ Feminism' Panel Discussion with Amy Richards,
Jennifer Baumgardner, and Gloria Steinem. San Francisco, 2000

Of Course You Can

"Ya know one day indigenous people of the
Earth are gonna reclaim what's rightfully theirs."
"Really? Uh-oh!"

Lose your mind misplace your mind
forgot you even had a mind
'cause someone told you it's impossible
to change your mind
a friend of mine made it to twenty-five
we had a celebration, "man I'm glad that you're alive"
I'm happy to see my man you're beatin' the odds
and for this on this day we give thanks to the gods
'cause everyone deserves a shot
except you only get one
I hope it's not through the head my son
'cause life is short when you're afraid to die
life is hard when you're afraid to cry
but when I feel alone I sing myself a song
because wherever I lay a groove is my home

    (chorus)
But can you see me in the desert?
of course you can!
can you see me on the mountain?
of course you can!
can you see me in the ocean?
of course you can!
I'm just splishin' and splashin'
and jumpin' in the sand!
        (repeat)

But he remembered memories of walkin'
through the puddles
sayin' "Gee dad, am I the one who's wanted by
the Federal Government
doesn't want me to go to school
I ask too many questions
and I don't play by their rules
in school they tried to tell me
that a rock is not alive
but I have seen a volcano growin' up and die
in school they tried to tell me
that a tree it couldn't feel
but I have felt a tree and it was bleeding for real
in school they tried to tell me

animals couldn't talk
but they can understand it when a dog starts to bark
in school they tried to tell me
man doesn't have a soul
"what happened to his" I say "'cause mine is still whole!"

    (chorus)
    (bridge)
"Can you see me?"
"can you see me?"

The reoccurring dream of a life's imprisonment
the reoccurring scream of a world and its residents
the reoccurring theme of a mind full of fingerprints
the reoccurring dream of a knife and a president
well would you like to look at Madonna's book on sex?
or would you rather Alex Haley's book on Malcolm X?
they're fuckin' with Ice T but they don't even care if
Eric Clapton's singin' I Shot The Sheriff!
but how many more books on this subject can I read
and how many more frustrations must I try to ease
and how many more days of this bad air can I breathe
and how many more of my friends must just die and leave

But you can't diffuse the ticking time bomb
you can't refuse the time it has come
you can't erase our people from the Nation
I'll take a life before they call us "the lost generation"

    (chorus)

Can you see me in Africa?
of course you can!
can you see me in Asia?
of course you can!
can you see me in Australia?
of course you can!
Aotearoa? Western Samoa? Eskimoa?
can you see me in the White House?
no you can't
can you see me on the radio?
hell no!
can you see me with the police?
in handcuffs?
splishin', splashin', jumpin' in the sand

HOLE IN THE BUCKET

(Money, money, money, money, nothing but money)
I work 9 to 5 but it starts in the P.M.
and I love the sunrise so I step out in the A.M.
the street is black and shiny from the early nightly rainin'
the glory of the light it brings evaporation
morning's fresh oxygen cleanest
I take a deep hit help my mind stay the greenest
I'm already wake so I'm not drinkin' coffee
don't wanna cigarette, 'cause it's a form of slavery
walk into the store 'cause I need a few items
the sun heats the blood like a hit of vitamins
needa buy some food and some 'poo for my dreads
can't remember why but I need a spool of thread
man with dirty dreads, steps around the corner
he asks me for a dime, a nickel or a quarter
I didn't have any change so I'm steppin' along
and as I'm walkin' past he sings to me a song...

      (chorus)
There's a hole in the bucket dear Liza, dear Liza...
      (repeat)

The day is pickin' up cause I'm hummin' his song
the buses and the people all keep movin' along
to the shopkeeper I say "was 'sup?"
and I'm thinkin' about the man who's holdin' up the cup
I pay for all the stuff and get a pocketful of change
should I give it to the man's the question in my brain
what's gonna happen if I give the man a dime?
I don't wanna pay for anotha brotha's wine
what's gonna happen if I give the man a quarter?
will he find a dealer and try to place an order?
what's gonna happen if I give the man a nickel?
will he buy some food or some pork that's been pickled?
I'm not responsible for the man's depression
how can I find compassion in the midst of recession?
how come all these questions keep fuckin' with my head
and I still can't rememba why I need a spool of thread

      (chorus)

He's starin' in my eyes just as I'm walkin' past
I'm tryin to avoid him cause I know he's gonna ask
me about the coinage that is in my pocket
but I don't know if I should put it in his bucket
walk right past him to think about it more
back at the crib I'm openin' up the door
a pocketful of change it don't mean a lot to me
my cup is half full but his is empty
I put back on my cap and I start headin' back
I reach into my pocket and I have a heart attack
well as I'm diggin' deep I scream "oh no!"
there's nothin' in my pocket but a great big hole
while I was busy thinkin' if he would buy smack
the jingle in my pocket it slipped through the cracks
no one has the change and it's fuckin' up my head
but now I know the reason why I had to buy the thread!

Michael on the corner of 16th and Valencia, outside of one of his favorite burrito shops (Taqueria La Cumbre) in the Mission district of San Francisco, 2000

HOME

If you are hungry I will
bake some bread for you
if you are worried I will
hold your head for you

If you can't sleep at night I will
screen your dreams for you

And if you feel uptight I will
make everything alright for you

If the key don't work
knock on the door
if the key don't work
knock on the door
no matter how far away you seem
I am always
here at home

(right) Jason Bell, Manas Itene, Ade' and Michael
laughing and chilling outside the Monopole Hotel.
A rare day off in Hamburg, Germany, 2001.

(above) Loading in at Secret Studios, 2000.

DREAM TEAM

Red Black Green, Red Gold Green
Dat's how we know we a fe we dream team
     (repeat)

The other day
a friend gave me a call
he said that the dream team was playin basketball
was so excited that I hadda get a witness
the first time the NBA was in the 'lympics
players from the East
players from the West
and you can bet that they took the very best
("Except they left Tim Hardaway at home"
"Yeah that was hella fucked up!")
but anyway
I tuned in because I was hella psyched
to see Magic Johnson on the same team as Mike
gettin' crazy havin lots of fun
but makin sure that they got the job done
fans were wavin' the red, white and blue
it seemed strange to me was it strange to you?
brotha's on the street and everyone is scared a ya
so how could ten Africans represent America?
bullshit it didn't mean a thing
'cause in the same year we saw Rodney King
so I thought that I would put a team together
a team that I have been waitin' for forever
some a you may know what I mean
but if you don't then
lemme introduce you to...
MY DREAM TEAM!
"SPEARHEAD IN THE AREA!"

     (chorus)
This is my dream team, my dream team
My dream team, my dream team

Well Chuck D's announcin' Flava's doin' color
halftime entertainment by Dre and Ed Lover
Malcolm X is the coach he's drawin' up the strategy
he's choppin up America's anatomy
'cause they're the ones we're up against of course
our general manager is Chief Crazy Horse
Huey Newton 'cause he was extra hard
he's the one who would be playin at the shootin' guard
and I dreamed Charles Barkley would be
played by Marcus Garvey
he'd be throwin people off his back and makin'
sure they never got a rebound rebound and
he'd throw it to the outlet

Nat Turner 'cause he can turn the corner
when he's out there he be flyin' through the air
throwin' passes like he really doesn't care
behind the back and in between the legs
he's handlin' the rock as gently as an egg
he's throwin' it in to Angela Davis's neighborhood
she's postin' up down in the extra hard wood
she grabs the pill and then she puts her shoulder down
get out the way 'cause she's gonna throw down now
boom oh my god! I just can't believe it
get anotha backboard or bettah yet leave it
we always play for fun but we always play for keeps
the game is over and the loser's gotta sweep
up the glass that we busted in the ass
set the record straight about America's past
THIS IS MY DREAM TEAM
"SPEARHEAD IN THE AREA!"

     (chorus)

Dream team is in the house
Dream team is in the house

Well after doin that we be headin' for the ceremony
hand on the heart is a bunch of baloney
the spirit of the '68 Olympics
Black Power people can I get a witness
fist in the air this is proper manners
while Jimi Hendrix is fuckin' up the spangled banner
up into the sky Miles Davis blows a horn
look into the bleachers it's Bill Clinton sellin' popcorn
so now we jump! and we have a celebration!
Shaquile O'Neal would provide the entertainment
to some of you this is a far fetched scheme
but to me...I'll tell you what it is...
this is my Dream Team...
"Spearhead in the area"

     (chorus)

Yeah Sista Rosa Parks she gets the first seat
on the bench!
and Dr. King, we bring him in in a pinch

Because I like to shoot hoops not brothas!
Because I like to shoot hoops not brothas!
Because I like to shoot hoops not brothas!
Because I like to shoot hoops not brothas!

Angela Davis and Michael discuss how they got involved
in activism at the Herbst Theater in San Francisco, 2002

Runfayalife

Every woman every man wanna move dem feet
every woman every man love a Spearhead beat!

Police in the city
is shuttin' all the clubs down
it's lookin' like a ghost town
ya know Mary what we gotta do?
"hell yeah!
we gotta go underground"
to da place from which we all came from
house parties–they was always fun
remember tryin' to rig a sound system
everybody would bring a donation
when we needed to get a turn table
my man Zulu
would borrow one from Aunt Mable
set it up in the corner
turn the lights down until the mornin'

      (chorus)
But the party ain't started till the speaker's blown
NO! NO! NO!
run fa ya life!
the party ain't started 'till the speaker's blown

While he was setting up camp
someone else would bring a home stereo amp
with a note from they mama
"don't turn it up loud or it's a goner"
sorry mama–there's no chance
cause if the shit ain't bumpin'
people ain't gonna dance
"know what I'm sayin'" ("Turn that shit up")
everybody in the place would bring a few speakers
string 'em all togetha like they was sneakers
and say a prayer–before we turn it on

hopin' that the amp wouldn't get blown
I asked Mary watcha think of it
"now we need a D.J. to work this shit"
so everybody would bring a few singles get
the beat bumpin'
and then start to mingle

      (chorus)

Every woman every man wanna move dem feet
every woman every man love a Spearhead beat!
every brother and every sister
would pay respect up to the ancestors
we would dance and we would celebrate
even though we live in a police state
then the pigs would try to make a statement
with a ticket for noise abatement
but we kept it pumpin' till the breakadawn
then we told the cops
they gotta break the door down
and today–across the nation–don't ya know
it's the same situation
alotta cities lookin' like a ghost town
but the house party will never be shut down
no, no, no!

      (chorus)

Every woman every man wanna move dem feet
every woman every man love a Spearhead beat!
      (repeat)

This one's dedicated to all the DJ's, rappers,
promoters, producers who continue to throw
jams in the face of adversity. Peace
Peace to the informal nation. Word Up!

*Michael, Dave Shul and RadioActive on the steps
of the Sydney Opera Hall. Sydney, Australia, 2001*

CRIME TO BE BROKE IN AMERICA

I take the needle off the record
and shove it in my arm
whenever I feel life is
comin' on too strong
they left me in a clinical fulla
cynical motha fuckin' bureaucrats
and other kind dingbats

Livin' on the tracks
the tracks in my arm said
it all depends which side the tracks your on
tellin' me what to wear
tellin' me cut my hair
and tryin' to convince me that they
really, really care
all about my health and about my wealth
but still they built the Stealth
'cause everybody's just lookin' out for they self
so then I ask 'em
can I have a clean needle
"Hell no that's illegal!"

    (chorus)
'Cause it's a crime to be broke in America!
and it's a crime to smoke dank in America!
    (repeat)

"Yeah hit those drums now"
they lockin' brother's in the poorhouse
who can't afford Moorhouse
politicians nervous
it's the only free service they provide
you wanna go inside
there's a hot meal waitin' for ya
a deal we can score ya
on a bed for a night or two
or three or four months

They say they lockin' us up in cells
to protect us from ourselves
it smells like they got anotha
plan in store house
or should I say warehouse
fulla niggas and other misfits
that couldn't turn tricks in the courthouse
it's a justice whorehouse

    (chorus)

Michael, San Francisco, 2001

It's a crime to be broke in America!
and it's a crime to be Black in America!
but there's a mutiny on the bounty
in every single county
we remember Attica
but don't forget to pat a few
others on the back as a matter of fact
sister Asatta Shakur and Geronimo Pratt
'cause Amnesty International
is fightin' for political
but if you're analytical
you know it's much more critical than that
percentages black is really, really whack
can I kick a few facts, yes?

Six percent in college
from livin' on the block
twenty-five percent in prison
the school of hard knocks
fifty percent in poverty
is livin' on the rocks
five hundred brothas on a death row box

The punishment is capital
for those who lack in capital
because a public defender
can't remember the last time
that a brother wasn't treated like an animal

they say they blame it on a song
when someone kills a cop
what music did they listen to
when they bombed Iraq?
give me one example so I can take a sample
no need to play it backwards
if you wanna hear the devil
'cause music's not the problem
it didn't cause the bombin'
but maybe they should listen
to the songs of people starving...

    (chorus)

'Cause it's a Crime to broke in America!
it's a crime to smoke dank in America!
it's a crime to be black in America!
it's a crime to be black in America!
it's a crime to be Puerto Rican
African
Native American
Asian, Hatian

100,000 MILES

I need a reason to get up before I wash my face
the junkies, the hookers, the dealers, the place
kickin' off my covers trippin' off the fact
that I haven't called my Gramma in a long, long time
standin' in the shower for almost half an hour
tryin' to wake up and I'm looking for the power
reachin' for the towel with soap in my eyes
dryin' off my shoulders my chest, and my thighs
the next thing I know the telephone rings
I hear my own voice on the answering machine
please leave a message I'm glad ya called
I listen for a voice but there's nothin' at all
man oh man
I gotta kick the blues
and pay respect where respect is due
all praises to GOD the one I return to
the one I can turn to
when I'm feelin' burned to the bone

   (chorus)
Early in the morn, before I wash my face
the bed is still warm but there's an empty space
early in the morn, before I wash my face
a hundred thousand miles is a lonely place

At six in the morning she rolled outa bed
stared out the window and then she said
that I wasn't her type...
I think she's runnin' outa types though...and I told her so
she picked up her things and walked through the door
and then said that she couldn't see me no more
just as she was leaving I asked her if she'd call
she didn't look back said nuttin' at all
I didn't change my clothes because they smell like you
and when I took a shower it reminded me of you
I called Gramma Brown for advice
it happened to me once it happened to me twice
Michael my son, you sound really bugged
I wish that you were here so I could to you give a hug
then she gave me a long, long talk
she said "you have the patience of ice on a sidewalk"

when things get rough don't sweat it
sometimes in life you just have to let it
and sing out a song so strong
that even a bad dream couldn't bring harm
to the mind of a young child's battles
formed from the candle light shadows
her voice is like a whispering kiss on the forehead

   (chorus)

In the last thirty minutes before I fall asleep
when I have said my prayers and I have brushed my teeth
this is the time when I am forced to think about
all the things I been tryin' to forget about
the bills, the phone, cleanin' up my room
the cars, the traffic, the speakers and the boom
alone I remember the times with me and you
and I realize my heart is shakin' up the room
Gramma she would tell us about the glory days
and Gramma she would tell us about when we were slaves
in the livin' room pianos outa tune
on top of it the pictures of every bride and groom
child, grand child, lost child
every single tear shed, every single smile
'cause everybodies got alotta shit to deal with
and life doesn't stop, it just makes ya feel it
so shake the dust offa your feet
take a step forward, liberate with the beat
so for you I wrote this song
I wanted you to hear it before you are gone
the African in me, the Seminole in me
these are some a things my grandmother gave to me
some believe there are and some believe there ain't
if ever there was one my Gramma Brown she is a saint

   (chorus)
Early in the morn, before I wash my face
the bed is still warm but there's an empty space
early in the morn, before I wash my face
a hundred thousand miles is a lonely place

Michael asleep on tour bus from Manchester, England to Dublin, Ireland. Sweaty, wet clothes (seen hanging to the left) are a part of everyday life on the bus and add to the charming, if not aromatic, ambience of life on the road. England, 2001

RED BEANS AND RICE

I don't eat red meat but I'm not a vegetarian
I like ice cream but not much dairy
'cause it gets in my nose
it makes me gotta blows
snot like a farmer and it gets on my clothes
it's rather unsightly, can even be frightening
but cold medication should not be taken nightly
because everything dat I put in, it comes out again
and if I eat lean, it helps me stay thin
check out my hair, I keep it dreaded
about my corn? I like it breaded
hot from the oven? MMM! you said it!
straight to the stomach, my fuel is unleaded
but not fossil fuels, I like olive oil
I like my eggs scrambled, I never eat 'em boiled
the way to my heart, is with a garlic clove
it smells hella sexy, when it's on the kitchen stove

(chorus)
Red beans and rice, red beans and rice,
red beans and rice, make everything nice
red beans and rice, red beans and rice,
red beans and rice, I could eat a place twice
so nice
so nice

Most people on the planet eat beans and rice
some can't afford beef or they think cows are nice
if you talk table manners, don't believe all they told ya
I eat with my fingers like an African soldier
I don't know which fork is for meat or for salad
I haven't got a clue when they say "whet your palate"
eat a lot a prunes it'll keep you loose
skin'll turn orange if you drink carrot juice
I think beef jerky tastes like a boot
when I'm on the street I chew a licorice root
and if I have a sore throat, then I eat ginger
and I will break bread with those who are strangers

so come into my cave, tonight I will show you
food is for life and life I will show you
If you're havin' problems, I invite you here
step into my kitchen, we will cook away your fears

(chorus)
Amazing grace how sweet the sound
that saved a wretch like me
damnit let's eat!
mi casa es su casa. Mi concina es su concina.
you know what I meana!

(bridge)
Get some boilin' water! Yeah!
get a pound of beans! Yeah!
get some spice and make it nice! Yeah!
you know what I mean!

But if a friend has gas, then he's passin'
it gives me a headache and I gotta take aspirin
it makes me dizzy, I fix him fizzies
to calm his stomach when it's feelin kinda busy
some like it white but I like it brown
I like spicy chicken and I can throw it down
chilies come red and chilies come green
when it's on the table, I lick my plate clean
then I drink a toast to the host and hostess
but first we give thanks to God the Mostest
'cause if I am a guest I always wash my plate
sip a sip a soda while I sing Amazing Grace
rings on my fingers left round the tub
bass fulla bubbles bumpin' like a wash tub
think about my troubles goin down the drain
dryin' up the puddles in the back of my brain
but...

(chorus)
(bridge)

Michael with Carl Young playing bass,
North Shore Lake Tahoe, 2001

CAUGHT WITHOUT AN UMBRELLA

Memories come down and me once again
caught without an umbrella
memories come down and me once again
caught without an umbrella

Well it was not that he was particularly
suicidal he just didn't care whether
he lived or died though
it was just a matter of time
you got yours and I got mine
when he turned sixteen
they said he could drive
when he turned eighteen they said he could die
when he turned twenty one he could buy rum
but no one ever taught him
how things were done
then an angel appeared inside his head
she said boy do you think
you're really better off dead
he don't know he just shook his head

     (chorus)
'Cause he thought the day that he died
would be a normal day for the people
on the other side
he thought that the day that he died
would be a normal day for the people
on the other side
but memories come down and me once again
caught without an umbrella

But time was a matter of velocity
in this age of information and technology
he would cry in the shower
put his face in a towel hot from the dryer
then he sat down and wrote a note to his mom
when all is said and done
can I still be your son
because manhood is so elusive
and respect is so exclusive

and I got a daddy to prove it
I think I'll never get to shake it and move
then he tied a rope around his neck
looked in the mirror and said what the heck
I'm gonna bring the whole roof down with me
and then he jumped

     (chorus)

"Come in Vernon"

But half way down
he heard what the angel said
and he realized he really didn't want to be dead
he landed with a thump–his head was reeling
layin' in a lump–looked up at the ceiling
and saw that the rope...had broke
well he failed at the only thing
that he thought he couldn't fail at
that was takin' his own life
and he said "I kinda like livin'"
he could feel his heart makin a boom
sounded like music in the next room
music in the next room
he said "it's time for a celebration"
felt his hands looked at his face
lifted the rope off his throat, "I ain't such a disgrace."
he said manhood is so elusive and respect is so exclusive
and I gotta daddy to prove, that some people
never get to shake it and move

     (chorus)

And he knew that the day that he tried
was not a normal day for the people

And memories come down and me once again
am caught without an umbrella

Michael in the rain. Portland, Oregon, 2002

CHOCOLATE SUPA HIGHWAY

1997

MADNESS IN THE ~~WORLD~~ HOOD KEEPS TRYIN'A
KILL THE VIBES
EVEN GRAMMAS PREACHER PACKS A 45
RUN GET THE CHALLICE
AND POSSE UP THE TRIBE
AND WITH THE LOVE OF RASTAFARI
WE SHALL NEVER DIE (STAY ALIVE)

Check IT!
THE SOUND REBOUNDING FROM THIS RECORD
AND GET IT ON DOWN Because Spearheads is 'bout
To wreck it AGAIN
MY FRIEND we'll make YOUR Body feel zen

gonna Rush ya head like ~~this~~ blood
AND change YA mood Like Heroin

Might
~~SOMETIMES~~ WE ~~DO GET~~ BITTEN WHEN DA BEAST
COMES TERRORIZIN
BUT LIKE THE SUN UP IN THE EAST WE KEEP ON RISIN'
EXPLODE
~~WE SMELL THE MUSHROOM CLOUDS ON DA HORIZON~~
~~NEW YEARS EVE 1999 WHAT WILL SAY TO ALL~~
~~THE THOUSANDS~~

POPS
Up in The morn unlock the liquor store ~~keys~~
HOOKERS ON Leavenworth ~~at the little up A horror~~
closin' up dey shops
COPS-LOOKIN Like A Blind cyclops
top
cuzhe ~~steals~~ ten percent of the cream off the ~~block~~
lickin plenty money smokin' down da pipe
~~we got~~ ~~three piece~~ who got a Piece last nigh

CHOCOLATE SUPA HIGHWAY

(chorus)
Rock rock y'all Spearheads comes alive
on the eve of two triple o
eleven forty-five
no jive we be survivin'
singin' praises to Jah
every time we throw down and every time we puff La
Haaaa!!!, well you can roll my way
on the chocolate supa highway!!!

Late last year
some of ya mighta had fear, that the Spearhead crew
would never be back through your way, no way
we naw go out like that, because we livin' for the riddim
and the funk is always fat so
we bring phat beats like a gift for Christmas
I'll make you testify just like an O.J. Simpson witness
our sound is so alarming like killer bees people all be swarming
so like the price is right come on down, make a little wish
but excuse me while I light my spliff and make some noise
if you think the herbs a gift. Hooo!

(chorus)

Check it I'm descending back into this record
the heavy breathing funky rhyme paramedic
shootin' funky venom from my sharp teeth injectors
not vex ya but yes to resurrect ya
'cause I can't stand the pain outside my window
why ya think so many smokin' indo blunts
sippin' gin and juice for confidence
blowin' more la than Jackie Chan be doin' stunts
the Buddha elevates the stress off the chest
but could never elevate boot off the ghetto necks
flex like flash when they try to pull me under
but like the lightnin' I'll be there before the thunder

(chorus)

Yes I remember the time in Oklahoma
you tired to blame an Arab
but the whitey was the bomber
you be jumpin' to conclusions
I think you spent your whole life
watchin' cable in seclusion
illusions 'bout what's outside your door
one nigga two nigga three nigga four
robbing every house and every liquor store
run for your life we marchin' one million more
plowing the fields like some natty dread farmers
you can roll your own in September from our harvest
big up yourself...when life comes gets the hardest
Spearheads comin' straight from the cartridge

(chorus)

(previous page) An early original draft of "Madness
In Tha Hood" from Chocolate Supa Highway, 1996

Session with George D. and Micky P. at the Record
Plant, Sausalito, 2001

KEEP ME LIFTED

(chorus)
So I gotta get lifted! All night yea, yea!
(Hip Hop business lift up America)
keep me lifted
(Hip Hop business lift up America)
so I gotta get lifted! All night yea! yea!
(you remind me of my herb you keep me lifted!)
keep me lifted!

I'm the dread lock producer
some call me Medusa
salaams and shaloms introduce ya
a rooster waking up the whole coopsta
Spearheaded man him nice haffe move ya
sshh...understand why we sweatin'
makin' love in the wake of Armageddon
forgettin'–Babylon need a lesson
drop the tech and use my tongue as a weapon
listen–I come to lubricate the friction
sound system purrin' with my diction
Frantz Fanon the Wretched of the Earth home
Phenomenon be goin' on and on
sailing along a likkle song
by the record take it home and fling it on

(chorus)

Hey yo I am the glory-fied of the story
child of a high crime rate category
they explore connect me to an I.Q. test
like a rat in a cage I'm trapped with the rest projects
but now I make my life go flip
like Malcolm comin' out the pen and shit

upliftment from a triflin' scene
to make a blind man murder for the things he seen
to believe is different than the daily bear witness
the spots filled up with the cocaine business
bullets trigger be pulled by the beast
kids paralyzed from his neck to his feet layin' way low
smokin' more and more...
seein' shapes in the chipped paint of my frame window
with slow visions of me livin' in the future
with forty, forty acres, acres and a Land Cruiser

(chorus)

Alpha-betical ABCD's come gettable
the brown brotha with the tone unforgettable
it's edible, every word be gourmet-able
Mecca Lekka shake ya hiney ho incredible
really though ya gettin' sick it when ya hear it so
I'm bringin' with it biorhythmical medical
anti-always dope my biotic
macrobiotic organic narcotic
the hemp is Kemp, like Kemp on hemp
super like the Sonics keep it real like rent so
tic tac toe me say all in a row
donkey want water me say "hold him joe"
my stereo killed the video star just like Arsenio Hall
so tall like the rain I never back fall
young lifted and black y'all

(chorus)

Performing at Leoncovello, Milan, Italy, 2001

FOOD FOR THA MASSES

I love family
'cause family brings inspirations
one love to you and peace to all the nations
Aztlan the Puerto Rican and Jamaican
African the Maori, Kouri and the Haitian
on the chocolate reservation
I'll take a hit and then pass the information
to the left hand side and
keep providin', pride and, sustenance and guidance
mass hysteria fools breaking down the barrier
militant cliques big up the area
put your fist n the air now,
show me that cha care now
and that cha really know how
don't get thee behind me Satan
I'll keep theee in front so I can kick thee in the ass and
assassinate all your wicked inventions
your new world order and your global intentions
not to mention the department of corrections
makin's money off of people in detention
doin' time for possessions
countin' the days in the dark they buildin' up aggressions

progressions all the dirty lessons
in the belly of the beast only God hears confessions
Geronimo Pratt's still sittin' in the cellar
done as many years as they did Mandela
parole board wanted to know are you remorseful
how could I be because I didn't do the crime yo
y'alls the motha fucka's that's guilty
lockin' me in solitary eight years of filthy
kill the messenger, you can't kill the message
yo I'm bringin' food for the masses

(chorus)
For the masses for the masses
mental food food for the masses
for the masses for the masses for the true for the true

So let's eat have a seat call the Maitre D'
commencin' with the riddim
I get open on the beat
let 'em say what they say about the way that we be
it's the new year two triple O they can't stop we
aw'ight, Sellassie I the book unfolds

(opposite) *A sea of hands at the 4th annual 911/Power to the Peaceful Festival in Golden Gate Park San Francisco, 2002*

(above) *Silhouette of Michael embracing Woody Harrelson at the 2001 Power to the Peaceful Festival. Dolores Park, San Francisco, 2001*

I write 'cause half the story has never been told to
no one can stop it in the whole world's droppin' out the socket
blowin' up, like NASA when I rock it
the high tech ways of the civilized man
can't stand my people but ya love a sun tan
fly the space shuttle like dancer and prancer
you nuke the North pole now you got skin cancer
the answer you see I'm fly like Lufthansa
you can Valujet but you takin' big chances on crashes
change your name like Cassius
the classes be making food for the masses
then shift to a speed that's common for the listeners
MC's and wanna be street politicians
in competition with the envious visions
they chasin' paper dollars to a pop chart prison
but listen this isn't me against you
'cause the whole world's checking out the things that we do
ya sold your soul to the Saint Ide's brew
that's awright I like the Sprite in you

   (chorus)

U Can't Sing R Song

Do you remember
all those days
the way that you loved me
in all those subtle ways
I can remember before you were gone
how when we heard our favorite song on the radio
you'd smile at me and sing along

(chorus)
But you can't sing our song
for no other lover
but you can't sing our song
for no other love

You and me would go dancin' after dark
long hot kisses and summer wishes in the park
New York
detail the car I never show up dirty
on colored people's time
I'd pick you up at 11:30 late night
we'd roll my hooptie down the boulevard
bumpin' bass and rolling low like we was superstars
killing me softly with the way you whisper in my ear
come here my dear
they're playing songs from back in yesteryear
the slow Jammer
the night programmer
the time to get undressed and where pajama slammer
the car antenna...
picks up songs that belongs to us like birds of feather
like heatwave on scratchy forty five
always forever

(chorus)

I was blind too blind to see
I took for granted the dope shit that you did for me
I mistook all your lovin' for captivity
like Ghetto boys I think my mind was playing tricks on me
I always wanted to let you know
like Aretha Franklin you sing just like the queen of soul
too many secrets in my heart I couldn't let it show
know I still want you and I'm sad we had to let it go...

(chorus)

Michael at the Sugar Shack, San Francisco, 2002

THA PAYROLL (STAY STRONG)

Gramma this one's for you (stay strong)

> *(chorus)*
> *He's strong!*
> *Mama, Mama, Mama, Mama I couldn't say "No"*
> *so strong!*
> *got sick and tired of seein' brothers being treated ill*
> *he's strong!*
> *they say to chill, they say my homey's not available*
> *stay strong!*
> *I hear Mama they got him working on tha payroll*
> *she's strong!*
> *Mama, Mama, Mama, Mama I couldn't say "No"*
> *so strong!*
> *got sick and tired of seein sistas being treated ill*
> *she's Strong!*
> *they say to child, they say my homegirl's not available*
> *stay strong!*
> *I hear Mama they got her workin' on tha payroll*

At 21 the brother "Smooth" he got a record deal
been working hard been writin' songs about the things he feels
he says it's real, 'cause I got the skills, but I got bills
my deck is stacked, if I could only get my shit on wax
when it was ripe he took his tape up to the rec execs
they smoked cigars and rolled their eye's at him behind their specs
your shit is phat but I don't hear it in the format Jack
what's all this black crap check page twenty one of your contract

> *(chorus)*

A friend of mine Roberta she got a job at the post office
she was college edjamacated but got fired up at the law office
I'm all alone two kids at home, I need a job just any job
so I can get back on my feet like Tina "T"(Turner)
the boss came up to her said, "Why don't you come home with me"
I'd like to see you take off your clothes for me
she said "No way man!"
he said "You don't understand"
"You lose your life, you lose your job if you don't do this shift!"

> *(chorus)*

I met a black man who became a police officer
officer, officer, officer, officer, officer, overseer
he tried to tell me it was the only job available
either rob or join the mob 'cause I'm not salable
one night he went out on an undercover sting-ing
bought some smack tried to break the heroin ring-ring
two cops white cops saw juggling going' down
they spilled the brain like homey the fuckin' clown
he's gone!
Mama, Mama, Mama, Mama I couldn't say no
got sick and tired of seein' people bein' treated ill
picked up my nines, walked up from behind
tapped two of them on the neck so I could meet their eyes direct
Pom! Pom!
I didn't do it for this payroll

> *(chorus)*

Michael on the beach in
Santa Cruz, California, 2002

MADNESS IN THA HOOD (FREE RIDE)

Ooh Ooh take a chance on a free ride
Ooh Ooh take a chance on a free ride free ride

Madness in tha hood keep trying to kill the vibes
even Gram's preacher packs a .45
run get the chalice and posse up the tribe
and with the love of Rastafari we shall never die

Wake up in the morn unlock the store pops
hookers on Leavenwort closing' up shops
cops, lookin' like a blind cyclops 'cause
they clockin' ten percent of the CREAM off the top
got mad money comin' down the pipe
from the three piece suit who gotta piece last night
the butcher the baker phony credit card maker
plus the operation being sponsored by Jamaica
and then there's the dime a dozen hoodie hitmen
who be killin' for sport, they got kids to support
slingin' dice come cross the snake eyes
come and take a chance on a free ride

> *(chorus)*
> *Badi ah-dee adi ah*
> *come and take a chance on a free ride*
> *badi ah-dee adi ah*
> *come and take a chance on a free ride*
> *ooh, ooh take a chance on a free ride*
> *madness in tha hood keeps tryin' a kill the vibes*
> *ooh, ooh take a chance on a free ride*
> *and with the love of Rastafari we shall never die*

Like Gregory Hines I return to the dance, dancin'!
broadcast vast audio radiance, enhance
wave hands, shake pants as I commence
D.J. wheel up drop bass then advance
I get reactions just like Johnny Cochran
when he compared Mark Fuhrman to that old German
listen Herman Munster was a gangsta
S.F.P.D. shield on his clothes gave up the answer
to the crack freak just released from jail
twenty in his pocket waitin' to inhale
takes deep breath from the piss stinkin' air
past the drag queen wearin' other people's hair
she snaps, "What you think you lookin' at here
you look like Jimmy Walker wearin' Biggy Small's gear
get the fuck away before I make you disappear
I don't play that freak shit do I make myself clear."

> *(chorus)*

During the "Sometimes" video shoot in Golden Gate Park,
San Francisco, 2001

Why Oh Why

I say my prayers every morning just like orange juice
I crack the crinkles out my body till I'm feeling loose
I strap my sneakers on my feet like they was combat boots
they fit my feet like Cinderella when I'm shooting hoops
why oh why do memories keep chasing me
sometimes it makes me wanna grab my shit and flee
sometimes I wanna blow my brains to put my life at ease
but I ain't checking out I gotta see the seven seas
please seven's a very lucky number for me
that was the age when I discovered how good balling could be
up every morning with the birdies doing little drills
go to my left go
to my right developing mad skills
how could a love for this game bring so much sadness
I played with brothas with so much badness
but now they gone I sing a song
pop a three from the top of the key in they memory

    (chorus)
Why oh why do memories be chasing me
sometimes it makes me wanna grab my shit and flee
even in seasons when it's another color sport
I still be memorizing lines out on the basketball court
singing why oh why do memories be chasing me
sometimes it makes me wanna grab my shit and flee
even in seasons when it's another color sport
I be remembering my partners on the basketball court

Do you remember runnin' the court in September
me and my homies be down for whoever
would come along and try to send us to the showers
from the game that we'd been dominatin' there for hours
all day to be more specific
East to West from Atlantic to Pacific
fools would come 'round to get down
and try to take our crown
but we would hold our ground and we would never back down
old timers new timers would get in line there
and take a seat there and try to prepare
but oh no! there was no chance when we was in the zone
we was alone at the top we had hops we got props
and when we needed to we busted chops
wipe the court with your game like we was using mops
whatever happened to the super hoopers
in the park I reminisce while shootin' solitary after dark

    (chorus)

Brother C. came fresh from out of town and
he had handles and like McDonald's he could clown ya
dribbling baby bounces between drinking forty ounces
knock ya on your heels and do circles like he was Curly Neal
but oh no, the liquor got quicker to his head and he said
"I think I musta placed some stupid bets"

Performing at the Ashland Armory,
Ashland, Oregon, 2000

he hit me up for some cash there was a car crash
a splash and then the brother made a mad dash
Rob oh Rob his whole life was like a roller coaster
but on the court he looked like a Dr. J poster
flying high with an Afro blowing in the wind
wiping Windex, index finger rolls
off the glass then swish through the net
jump a Corvette with a triple pirouette
but off the court he had a few temptations
copulations no moderations by 24 he had 3 pregnations
last check crack intoxications
so many other brothers gone from this dimension
and none of those who got hurt receive a pension
give a bup! bup! to those locked up in detention
memories too many dimension
and we say, one more time...one more time

    (chorus)

(right) Michael jumping at the Dunya fest in
Rotterdam Holland, 2001

COMIN' TO GITCHA

And the Lord spoke unto Moses,
"Go unto Pharoah, and say unto him
'Thus say the Lord,
let my people go, that they may serve me.
And if thou refuse to let them go,
behold, I will smite all thy border
with frogs...'"

(chorus)
I'm comin' to gitcha
I'm comin' to gitcha
I'm comin' to gitcha
I'm...comin'...to gitcha

Babe I'm sick and tired of bein' alone and
I call 911 up the phone and
you're like Ebola in my system
I'm sick with you but you're the serum
voo doo be tuggin' on my apron see and
I can feel Screamin' Jay Hawkins possessin' me and
damned in reckless abandon,
imagine suspended in the canyon

(chorus)

I don't understand I feel like I'm going crazy 'cause I
I wanna feel you in my...
I don't know what...I'm gonna do 'cause
I have these dreams
about followin' you with my hands...
and I get all nervous 'cause I...
I wanna call you up and I...

(chorus)

Baby makin' music for the massive
global telecommunication
Aboriginal Black Militia Broadcastin' system
the chocolate melter, the helter skelter
the skull rattler, the bush doctor
the part the Red Sea boom shocka
una bomber super jamma
jungle business melt in the mic not in your hand
Jah! master mind the master plan

(chorus)

*Michael on set of video shoot for "Sometimes." The video was
eventually scrapped but many unusual and humorous photos
were taken at the shoot. San Francisco 2001*

GANJA BABE

I wanna make it slow
sensemille
I wanna make it slow
make me feel ya

Heavy medicine
ya see my eyes are feeling red again
I'm bringin' light
like Thomas funky Edison

Been in the desert for forty seven days
purple haze
the poison that I tasted never changed
turn up the woofers so I can feel the beat
vibrate my belly like a bomb in a harmony
summer heat
my back is sticking to me to the seat
bare feet, tank top and shorts is all ya need
summer breeze
I'm feelin' kinda fine
I'm rolling with my shorty all the time
wind and grind lovely shake your behind
cinnamon skin be bringing sin to my mind
but whether or not the weather's hot
or the weather's cold
I'm wrapping her like a blanket with my whole soul
so that she can feel me
like Coca-Cola I'm the woo-o-oh oh the sweet thing
my girl lollipop she growing mad crops

she rollin' herbs everyday
at about 4 o'clock tick tock
strike the hammer while the iron's hot
ooh girl watcha got cooking in the pot
see Mary, Mary, Mary quite contrary
how does your garden grow
hydroponic ultra supersonic
or does it grow naturally slow

 (chorus)
Ganja babe my sweet ganja babe
I love the way ya love me and the way ya misbehavin'
ganja babe my sweet ganja babe
come wake body-ody take my mind away

Everybody get down and do the boogaloo
just like the cover of I want you
yoo hooo—look watcha gonna do
watcha gonna do when the rent comes due
round up the posse and call up the crew
5 bucks at the door and ya bring ya own booze
call ya neighbor 'cause they can come too
be sure and bring ya records 'cause I only got a few
so baa baa black sheep have you any wool
yes sir, yes sir a nickel bagful
one for my partner, one for ma crew
some for my ganja baby she needs 2
cuz just like me they want to be...cool

 (chorus)

Michael in Lake Tahoe, 2000

WAYFARIN' STRANGER

I'm just a poor wayfarin' stranger
travelin' through this world of woe
there's no sickness toil nor sorrow
in that bright world to which I go
I'm going there to see my father
I'm goin' there no more to roam
I'm just a going' over Jordan I'm just a going' over home

Ya see I'm a concrete buffalo soldier
I gotta chip it's like a boulder on my shoulder
look in my eyes and you can see a red marble
like Nostradamus I'm the promise of tomorrow
traveling the city with my Mexican cargo
cotton mouth–I take a dry swallow
to the nearest corner watering hole
the bartender with the deed for my soul
satisfaction no I can't get no
lotsa bad habits that I need to control
recite the Psalms but no emancipation
church for food and liquor stores for salvation
some day I'll make
it home to see my Father
he saw the man who shot the coal miner's daughter
and if I had a dime for every gamble I risked
I could buy a diamond for the woman I miss ya see

(chorus)
I'm just a poor wayfarin' stranger
ya check with me ya checking in with danger
I'm just a poor wayfarin' stranger
roaming the streets seeking Jesus in a manger

I'm goin' there to see my Mother
she said she'll meet me when I come

I'm just a going' over Jordan I'm just a going' over home
Jordan river roll, river Jordan roll, river Jordan roll on

Gee ain't it funny–how time slips away I wanna
rewind the tape to see my life replay
I soak up the sun–just as a reminder
that I was born a sick side winder
call me a vagrant, no machine to read your fax
I'll never pledge allegiance to your blood sweat and taxes
don't ever mistake me being docile for contentment
don't my anger for resentment

it's just the calm before the storm that's why I'm quiet
ya always mistaking an uprising for a race riot
you can take my life–but there's no escape
'cause you can't shoot yer way through the pearly gates
so swing low sweet Cadillac
coming for to carry me home
swing low pink Cadillac
stepping over Jordan I roam

I'm just a poor wayfarin' stranger
ya check with me ya checking in with danger
ya check with me ya checking in with danger
I'm just a poor wayfarin' stranger
roaming the streets seeking Jesus in a manger

(chorus)
When the road is callin' yonder, when the road is callin' yonder
when the road is callin', when the road is callin' yonder
I'll be there

(chorus)

*(left) Michael waiting to go onstage in the stairwell of the
historic King Tut's Wah Wah Hut. The ceiling above the
stage was so low that Michael jumped, he hit his head on
some pipes. The gig was so hot that the ceiling dripped water
onto the stage, causing another accident...Michael falling on
his ass! Glasgow, Scotland, 2001*

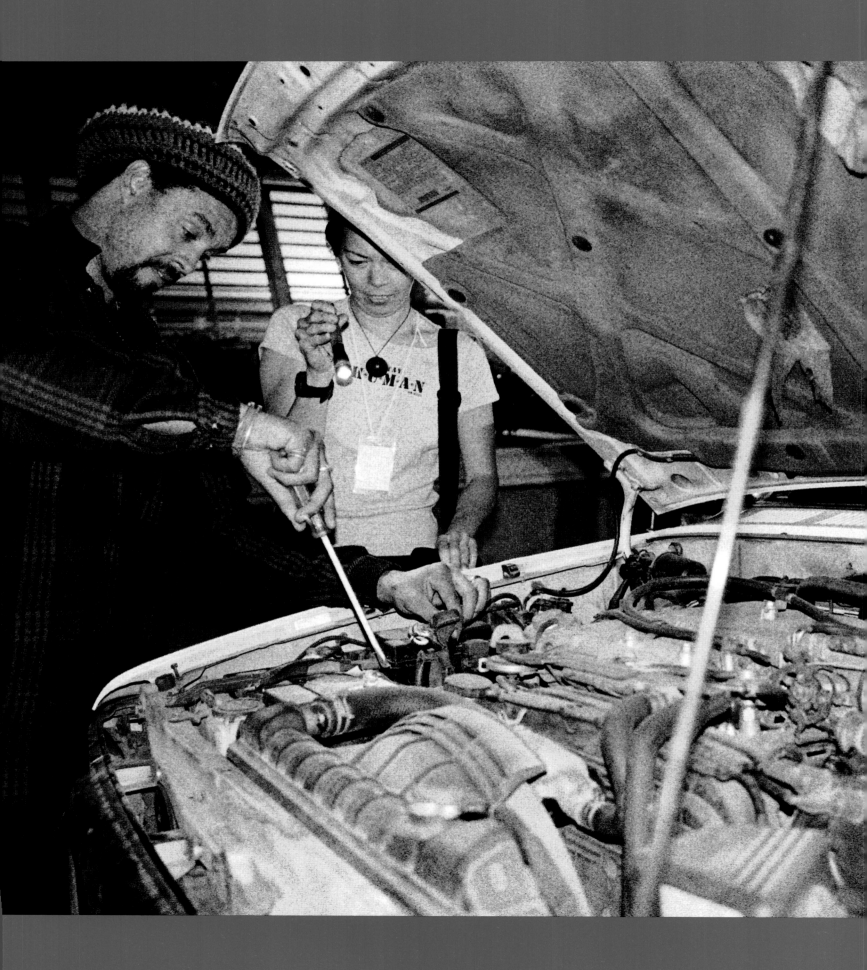

GAS GAUGE (THA WORLD'S IN YOUR HANDS)

At day's arrival
one man at the table
eatin' corn flakes
checkin' out the paper
his brother walks in from a hard nights caper
half hungover and looking for his pager
what's in the news today did we find a savior
nah I'm just looking for some part time labor by the way
did you remember put the gas in my ride
or must I remind ya how I lost my last job
chill with all that chatter
ya know ya need to stall
trust me baby bro that's what big brotha's for
uh uh, I got interviews today
so don't even front about my broken gas gauge
by the way things are looking it's a very good day
if I could ever find my wallet I'll be on my way
bigger brotha steps up to his girlfriend's place
just then the phone rings and it was moms to say
remind ya big brotha it's your cousin's birthday
and I'ma need a half dozen eggs for the cake
no problem moms I'll tell him later in the day
but now I can't find my wallet gotta go I'm late

(chorus)
*Tha world's in your hands
don't waste...don't waste your time*

Back to the saga
the car wouldn't start up jjjhhh...jjjhhh there he goes
now he's rolling like a baller
out of the city and into the woods
for a job with a hammer where the pay is good
reaches in the back seat for his favorite tape
uuuh a condom from his brotha's last date
damn my laze no good brotha
and just as he says it, the car starts to sputter
and sputter, until it outright stops
the gas tank empty, not even a drop
I'm gonna choke that nigga when I reach my spot
three miles from no place and now I gotta walk
to the top of the hill and down again
'round the bend page my brotha from the old fruit stand
the phone ring rings yo it's me your big brotha
I told ya not to sweat me when I'm laying with my lover
what! You punk ass broke muthafukka
I told ya cut the crap when it came to my endeavors
chill baby bro and don't even start it there's a gallon in

the trunk and if ya need more fart it
some of my shit along with ya lost wallet
is in the glove box kid, the mystery solv-en
take what's yours and leave mine where ya saw it
my baby's calling gotta go stay solid

(chorus)

so he hung up the phone in a rush to leave
I forget to tell my brotha 'bout the cake recipe
star 69 so he pushed it in
but by now the bigger brotha was pursuing some skins
the phone ring rings—don't answer it
it's my little brotha calling fuckin' with me again
so he beeped him back a one two more times
but he was already naked with his Valentine
damn—I gotta—get back to the ride what the hell's
going on with this day of mine,
once again up the hill down the other side
what the fucks a cop doin' snooping by my ride
yo officer—check it out everything is fine
I just ran outta gas and now I'm running outta time
slow down boy this ain't no race
I can tell you kinda people ain't from this place
tell ya what turn around put ya hands on the hood
and ya best act good just like a good boy should
listen up holdup—I'm speaking the truth
see I'm just trying to get to this here job interview
shut them lips boy don't let 'em get no bigger
or I'm gonna have to say I was attacked by a nigger
now if you wanna make it through the morning with me
I suggest you wise up and show me valid I.D.
chill man—awright—problem—we solve it
my brotha put my wallet in the glove box compartment
aw'right you can get it but ya don't move quick
just remember I'm behind ya with a full up clip
he opens the box and to their surprise
out pops a wallet and the bigger brothers nine
the cop shouts "Freeze"
raise ya hand kid he reaches for his wallet
and the cop goes blam
damn—pulp fiction in the car
another dead homey tryin' a finda job
mmm, mmm, mmm
back at the crib bigger brotha laying up and girlfriend says
maybe you should give ya little brother a call
and don't forget it's ya cousin's birthday after all
I will in a minute please let me be
I think he left me a message on the message machine
big brotha—I'm gonna be home late
and I'm afraid that my day hasn't been great
can I remind you if it's not too late
to get a half dozen eggs for the birthday cake

*Michael and his manager Catherine Enny doing what artists
and managers often do. Attempt to fix things that don't work.
This time they were successful at starting Michael's car and
just barely made it from a speaking engagement with feminist
activist Gloria Steinem at San Francisco's Herbst Theater,
to Spearhead's gig at The Fillmore. San Francisco, 2000*

STAY HUMAN

2001

ALL THE FREAKY PEOPLE
MAKE THE BEAUTY OF THE WORLD

STARVATION IS A CREATION OF THE DEVIL
A REBEL I'M BRINGING FOOD THE PEOPLE
~~IN THE MIDDLE~~ LIKE A WIDOW
BRINGIN FLOWERS TO ~~A~~ GRAVE IN THE MIDDLE
OF THE CITY ISOLATION IS A RIPPLE???
TO BE SURROUNDED BY A MILLION OTHER
 PEOPLE BUT FEEL ALONE LIKE A TREE
IN THE DESERT DRIED UP LIKE THE SKIN
OF A LIZARD BUT FULLA COLOR LIKE
THE SPOTS OF A LEOPARD. DRUM AND BASS
PULL ME IN LIKE A SHEPERD/SCRATCH
MY ITCH LIKE A NEEDLE ON A RECORD
~~DON FULLA LIFE LIKE A MAN GONE TO MECCA~~ ~~CATCH LIGHT AND REFLECT IT~~
SKY HIGH LIKE AN EAGLE UP SOARING
I SPEAK LOW BUT I'M LIKE A LION ROARING
BARITONE LIKE A ROBESON RECORDING
I'M GIVING THANKS FOR BEING HUMAN
EVERY MORNING
 CAUSE THE STREETS ARE ALIVE!!!
WITH THE SOUND OF BOOMBAP!
CAN I HEAR IT ONCE AGAIN BOOMBAP
TELL YOUR NEIGHBOR TELL A FRIEND
EVERY FLOWER GOT A RIGHT TO BE BLOOMIN
EVERY BOY GOT A RIGHT TO BE BOOMIN!
 STAY HUMAN!

Oh My God

Slam bam I come unseen
but like gasoline you can tell I'm in the tank
like money in the bank
I smell appealing, but I'm toxic, can send ya reeling,
without an inklin', keep ya thinkin'
'cause you gave cash to the feds, left your school district for dead
fucked you up in the head, but still they sayin' nothin's wrong
sellin' firewater but outlawing the bong
still believing the system is workin'
while half of my people are still outta workin'
anonymous notes left in the pockets and coats
of judges and juries from 'Frisco to Jersey
threats and protests politicians mob debts
trumped up charges and phony arrests
stage a lethal injection, the night before the election
'cause he got donations from the prison guard union

(chorus)
Oh-my, oh-my God!
out here mama they got us livin' suicide
singin' oh-my, oh-my God!
out here mama they got us livin' genocide

Listen in to my stethoscope on a rope
internal lullabyes, human cries
thumps and silence, the language of violence
algorithmic, cataclysmic, seismic, biorhythmic
you can make a life longer, but you can't save it
you can make a clone and then you try to enslave it?
stealin' DNA samples from the unborn
and then you comin' after us
'cause we sampled a James Brown horn?
scientists who's God is progress
a four headed sheep is their latest project

the CIA runnin' like that Jones from Indiana
but they still won't talk about that (Jim Jones
People's temple mass killing) in Guyana
this ain't no cartoon
no one slips on bananas
do you really think that that car killed Diana
hell I shot Ronald Reagan, I shot JFK,
I slept with Marilyn (Monroe) she sung me happy birthday
singin'

(chorus)

Well politicians got lipstick on the collar
the whole media started to holler
but I don't give a fuck who they screwin' in private
I wanna know who they screwin' in public
robbin', cheatin, stealin',
white collar criminal
McDonald eatin', you deserve a beatin'
send you home a weepin', with a fat bill for your
Caribbean weekend
for just about anything they can bust us
false advertising sayin' "halls of Justice"
you tellin' the youth don't be so violent
then you drop bombs on every single continent
mandatory minimum sentencin'
'cause he got caught with a pocket fulla medicine
do that again another ten up in the pen
I feel so mad I wanna bomb an institution
singin'

(chorus)

(previous page) Original draft of the song
"Stay Human" from the album Stay Human, *2000*

Manas Itene (Spearhead drummer), Michael, Carl Young, and Papa Pretty (aka Albert Cooke Spearhead's tour manager) take time out from their European tour to visit Nuengamme Concentration Camp. They are shown here standing in front of one of thousands of train cars used to haul Jewish prisoners during the Holocaust. Ironically, today the camp is the site of three active prisons, one maximum, one medium and one minimum security facility. At the time of the visit, a group of survivors and volunteers at the museum were working to have the prisons closed, because they felt it was a disgrace to the memory of those who died there to continue to run the site as a modern prison.

STAY HUMAN

Starvation is a creation of the devil, a rebel
I'm bringin' food to the people like a widow
bringin' flowers to a grave in the middle
of the city isolation is a riddle
to be surrounded by a million other people
but feel alone like a tree in the desert
dried up like the skin of a lizard
but full of color like the spots of a leopard
drum and bass pull me in like a shepherd
scratch my itch like a needle on a record
full of life like a man gone to Mecca
sky high like an eagle up soaring
I speak low but I'm like a lion roaring
baritone like a Robeson recordin'
I'm givin' thanks for bein' human every morning...

        (chorus)
Because the streets are alive with the sound of boom bap
can I here it once again!
boom bap tell your neighbor tell a friend
every box gotta right to be boomin'
because the streets are alive with the sound of boom bap
can I here it once again!
every flower gotta right to be bloomin'!
stay human!

Be resistant
the negativity we keep it at a distance
call for backup and I'll give you some assistance
like a lifesaver deep in the ocean

stay afloat here upon the funky motion
rock and roll upon the waves of the season
hold your breath and your underwater breathin'
to be rhymin' without a real reason
is to claim but not to practice a religion
if television is the drug of the nation
satellite is immaculate reception
beaming in they can look and they can listen
so you see don't believe in the system
to legalize you or give you your freedom
you want rights ask 'em, they'll read 'em
but every flower gotta right to be bloomin'...
stay human...

        (chorus)

You see Y2K ya know is a moment
in time we find that we can open
up a heart that's locked or been broken
by the pain of words not spoken
or shot by guns a still smokin'
Cartwrights out on the Ponderosa
or drive by bang in Testarossa
we need to heed the words of Dali Lama
or at least the words of yo mama
take a mental trip to the Bahamas
steam your body in a stereo sauna, sauna, comma...

        (chorus)

Michael at a press conference upon arrival
for the "Stay Human" Tour in Melbourne, 2001

ROCK THE NATION

We livin' in a mean time and an aggressive time
a painful time, a time where cynicism rots the vine
in a time where violence blocks the summer shine
lifetimes, go by in a flash
in a search for love, in a search for cash
everybody wanna be some fat tycoon
everybody wanna be on a tropic honeymoon
nobody wanna sing a little bit out of tune
or be the backbone of a rebel platoon
it's too soon to step out of line
you might get laughed at you might get fined
but do you feel me when I say I feel pain everyday
when I see the way my fiends gotta slave
and never get ahead of bills they gotta pay
no way no way!
some make a living doing killing Colombian penicillin
some are willing to play the villain they just chillin'
to pass the time, pass the information
or pass the wine
pass the buck or pass the baton
but you can't pass the police or the Pentagon
the I.R.S. or the upper echelon
I think it's time to make a move on the contradiction

> *(chorus)*
> *Bom-bom, rock the nation*
> *take over television and radio station*
> *bom-bom the truth shall come*
> *give the corporation some complication!*

This is the dawning of our time I say it one more time
to emphasize the meaning of my rhyme
to rise above all the dirt and grime
add the right spice at the right time
fuck the constitution
are we part of the solution or are we part of the pollution
sittin' by and wonderin' why,
things ain't the way we like to find them to be, to be
for you and to me the people over there and the ones in between
check our habitation are we a peace lovin' nation
peace lovin' nation
I have a reasonable doubt I think I'll just spell it out
there's no need to scream or to shout
the N.R.A. just bought a man's soul
then he jumps up and shouts gun control
the government says that killin's a sin
unless you kill a murderer with a lethal syringe
so I ask again "are we peace lover's then"
some of them slang guns when they six years old
some of them end up in a six foot hole
this whole damn place seems to, lost control
so I raise my voice before I lose my soul

> *(chorus)*

Michael with Aboriginal youth dancers at Womeera Aboriginal College. Michael's son Cappy is seen in the top right corner of the photo, 2001, Healsville, Australia, 2001

Shadows of the show at the Fillmore, San Francisco, CA, 2001

SOMETIMES

(chorus)

Sometimes, I feel like I can do anything and
sometimes, I'm so alive
sometimes, I feel like I can zoom cross the sky and,
sometimes, I wanna cry

Most people try to aim to please
but a lot a them are kinda weak in the knees
learnin' late about the birds and the bees
fallin' in love and wanna be set free
playin' ball at the age of thirteen
everybody's growin' up with a dream
I never noticed what could happen to me
time flies when you're walkin' the streets
one minute gotcha holdin' an ace
the next minute gotcha fall on yer face
a mean city is a nasty place
only a rat can win a rat race!
peace to the people who be fallin' away
to make it home today
and peace to the people who be tryin' to find
some kinda life

(chorus)

Sound body and sound of mind
sound of the rhythm and sound of the rhyme

somebody marchin' all out of time
biggest mistakes are the humanest kind
judge not, lest you be judged
the court room or the billy club
blood bubblin' thicker than mud
the heart beat rub-a-dub-dub
show love and love who you know
family wherever you go
Tokyo to Acapulco
bravissimo, magnifico
peace to the people who be losing their head
peace to the people who be needin' a bed
love to the people who be feelin' alone
spreadin' love upon the microphone
hope to the people who be feelin' down
smile to the people who be wearin' a frown
faith to the people who be seekin' the truth y'all
all of the time, and i say

(chorus)

Ya know I'll come for you
ya know I'll come for you
ya know I'll come for you
ya know I'll come for you

DO YA LOVE

So many times, people turn they backs to you
'cause they don't wanna see, what's inside of you
'cause lookin' inside of you
they might realize there's something inside of them
they might night not wanna find
but it ain't about who ya love
see it's all about do ya love

(chorus)
Well well well well
sunshine, and loveliness,
ain't nobody feeling no ugliness
ain't it fine like sippin sweet Georgie wine
see I'm just chillin' with these friends of mine

I ain't tryin' a bother you
so why ya gotta bother me
what goes on in your bedroom ain't no mess to me
you say your God don't like my God
'cause you don't like my friends
but your friends tryin' to kill a man
and I don't understand
'cause it ain't about who ya love, (who ya love)
see it's all about do ya love, (do ya love)

(chorus)

Ooh one two three
say yeah say yeah feels so good to me
ooh! and ya one two three, say yeah, say yeah
feels so good!!!!

I say do it at home or on the street
with a drag queen don't matter to me
it ain't about sex or having degrees
your pedigree don't matter to me
it ain't about who ya love
see it's all about do ya love

(chorus)

Michael at soundcheck in Dublin, Ireland, 2001

Cappy Franti (age 14) Michael and Ade' Franti-Rye (age 2) sit for a television interview at the Splendor in the Grass Festival. Byron Bay, Australia. 2001

SOULSHINE

The world around
gotcha down
you got high blood pressure, people pushin' you around
and some wanna tell you how you should behave
cut your hair the right way, tell you what to say
hang out with the right folks
become a fashion slave

But do you wanna feel free
but do you wanna feel freaky and free
but do you wanna feel free
do you wanna feel free, free, free, freaky and free!

     (chorus)
Take ya time
Unwind ya mind
We all need a little soulshine
Take ya time
Unwind ya mind
We could use a little soulshine

9 to 5, people tryin'a stay alive
hard livin' in the city
find a diamond in the sewer but the gas bills rise
but I got to say to them what's it all mean
ya got to take a loan
to pay the bill on the phone
educated, graduated but you can't get a job

But do you wanna feel free
but do you wanna feel freaky and free
but do you wanna feel free
do you wanna feel free, free, free, freaky and free!

EVERY SINGLE SOUL

No matter where I roam
whoa-oh I know every single soul is a poem
written on the back of God's hand

Ya see Moms and Pops be copulatin'
plantin' seeds and pickin' weeds for another season
another reason for livin' another reason for givin'
another reason for lovin' and tryin'a stay out of prison
'cause everything in life can't be nice and
everything you want can't be got
but the lessons on being patient be causing the pressure to rise
and make some people suicidal
Oh no! another soul; has lost control
we pull him back into the fold
he got strung out on the material
all the superficial initials
upon his clothes
they make me wanna go Sprewell
every time I see my family locked in jail
uh-huh, the economic can be demonical oh!
keep love in your soul

   (chorus)

Ya see people are so beautiful in love
that's why I'm reminded of life every morning every time

I see lovers walkin' by in the park
clothes my eyes and I stop reminisce
to see a little baby suckin' on his mama's
milk-ey silky smoothness of a lovin' caress holdin' baby to breast
and blessin' the world with another to test, test, test
oh-yes, oh-yes bom-bom!
I'd like to sing a little song
dedicated to the people who would like to sing along
'cause every little song has little beats and notes
like every little lake has little trees and boats
all people deserve a safe and warm home 'cause every single soul is a poem

   (chorus)

Right from the start in a world torn apart
a baby's love leaves finger prints upon the heart
so many think it, but never say it
"why bring a child to this planet full of hatred"
they might not make it like the youngest departed
or worst of all they might become a part of it
involved in it, perpetuating violence, violence
and growin' up in silence... seein' things they don't know how to deal with
and learnin' ways, to try to cope with it,
cope with it, cope with it.....and not lose hope

   (chorus)

Ade' points to a poster of Dad in
Munich, Germany, 2001

Michael hugs Saul Williams after performing "Every Single Soul" together in
The Commodore Ballroom. Vancouver B.C., Canada, 2002

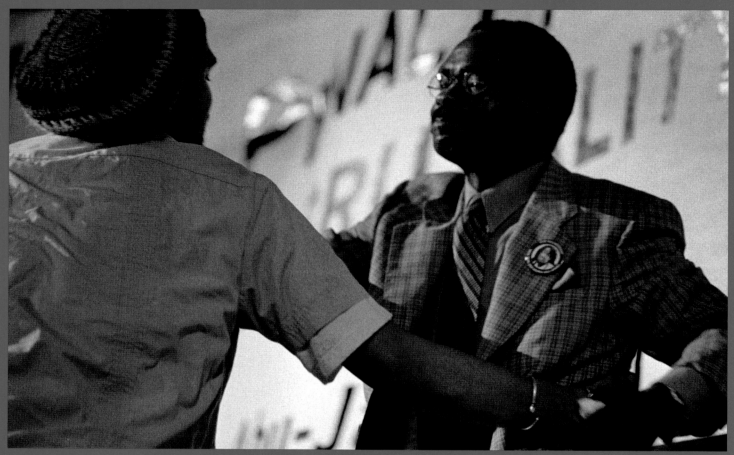

Michael greets World Champion Middleweight Boxer, Rubin "Hurricane" Carter at a fundraiser for Mumia Abu Jamal. Carter was exonerated and released after serving 19 years in prison (11 in solitary confinement) for a murder he did not commit. He was the subject of the Bob Dylan song "Hurricane" and Denzel Washington received an Oscar nomination for his portrayal of him in the 2000 film of the same name. Mission High School Auditorium, San Francisco, 2001

LOVE'LL SET ME FREE

Seems like everyday gets a little bit longer
seems like yesterday I was a little bit stronger
but there ain't nothin'
nothin' left to do
but to hold my ground
try not to come unwound
don't wanna be let down
but it ain't easy, no!
doin' hard time
somebody else's crime

(chorus)
Hate is what got me here
but love, sweet love is gonna set me free
all the hatred in the world is what got me here today
but I know that love is gonna set me free

Man I been away for so long now
I ain't seen no daylight for God knows how long now
I come out fightin when I hear that bell ring
I always hear my name
but I'd love to feel the rain come down one more time
wash away my pain
love like a hurricane

(chorus)

Power to the Peaceful, Dolores Park, San Francisco, 2001

THANK YOU

When I was a younger man
people say don't dream to tall
if you live your life that way
you set yourself up for big falls
I stay up late in my room at night
play my heroes on the turntable
opened me to pure phat groove
help my soul break down them walls

(chorus)
I thank you
I thankin' you for all the music that you've shown to me
I thank you
you set me free
free to simply just be me

You don't know
all the influence
the subtle positives
you had on me
came about like a renaissance
but love love is gonna set me free a little happy dance
got into my feet
but in your time
the roads you choose
led you to your hard luck blues
I always feared what it was like
to live inside your big old shoes

(chorus)

Do ya love music? "I do!!!"
do ya love music? "I do!!!"

Michael barefoot on stage at a party for K2 Snowboards. He stopped wearing footwear of all types in April of 2000 and continues to go barefoot through all seasons except where it is legally required. Mount Baker, Washington, 2001. (opposite) Michael speaks to kids at The Environmental Middle School. Portland, Oregon, 2002

We Don't Mind

We don't mind
see we been doin' it all the time
but if you want us to sacrifice
you will not get it without a price
we don't mind
see we been doin' it all the time
but if you want us to sacrifice
you gotta give something back to life

You think I'm vulnerable to your pressure tactics
because I shed a tear, 'cause I shed a tear
you think I'm vulnerable to your violence
just 'cause I'm sittin' here
but my babies came into this world
without a single fear, say they had no fear
'cause the seven generations before me
they all fought to get us here

     (chorus)

You can't just come in here like that no more
and snatch up our childhood
you can't just walk on up
and replace it yo, with your Hollywood
but I see now
how all of the words I say you'll take and misconstrue
and I'm prepared now
to suffer the penalties for speakin' the truth
and I speak the truth when I say

     (chorus)

People if you hear me now I wantcha to say
naa, na-naa, na-naa, naah
people if you hear me now I wantcha to say
naa, na-naa, na-naa, naah

SPEAKING OF TONGUES

You don't have to be so scared to share what's inside
'cause you're Daddy's little superstar,
and you're mama's little butterfly
fly high...

A strange strange litany of verses and reverses
ad-libs and rehearses
clouds burst and words cursed
an argument breaks out
it's one we've all heard before, it's boring
had us all snoring from the first line
one after another chimed in perfect time
tired rehashes of petty cashes and mismatches
you shoulda coulda's
and "why didn'tcha dida's"
crippling snippets aimed at the heart
to inflame and impart blame
framed like Mumia
verbal diarrhea spasms
creating chasms between the souls of two
or two billion
nations torn apart,
station to station damnation,
with much deliberation and very little consideration
to the return on the damage from the altercation,
collateral condemnation,
then denyin' like colorization of an old black and white
create a revision of the recent last night
the fight that started with two words "I'm right."

(chorus)
You don't have to be so scared to share what's inside
'cause you're Daddy's little superstar, and you're Mama's little butterfly
fly high...

But of course the fight ends with no resolution.
merely a vow for retribution, substitution, execution, electrocution
ruthless, toothless, and truthless
mumbling through page after page of excuses
abuses of the gift of gab
Gabriel the trumpeter
bestowed upon us a voice with a choice,
and a tongue kept moist by years of salivating
for oysters...pearls and aphrodisiac's
locked in an ugly shell always too chewy and gooey
so they get swallowed whole,
but a tongue is so much more than a vehicle for greed
or the decipherer of feed,

A tongue is for washing fur
or for licking wounds
or for welcoming new comers into a room,
or cleansing those fresh from the womb
without a tongue there'd be no croons,
swoons, Junes under the moon,

no bees pollinating no flowers to bloom,
no recitation of words at the foot of a tomb
or wills red allowed of the family heirlooms
you probably couldn't even blow up a balloon,
and that would be a shame
because to exhales the name of the game
exhale from the heart, not from the lungs
speak from the heart, not from the tongue

(chorus)

Listening is understanding
and finding compassion, love is the action
of soul satisfaction
a tongue can make wishes and also fine kisses
taste a sweet cake and also cast disses
but nothing compares to the voice from within,
without it we might just be mannequins,
up to no darn good shenanigans
learn to be skillful movers of the stones
that block the heart and turn humans to clones
learn to forgive, set free the bones,
touch with your flesh, take off the rubber gloves
love like your life depends on it
because it does!!!!!!

(chorus)

LISTENER SUPPORTED

Six foot six above sea level
I grab the mic because I like to take you to
anotha mental level
low power frequency radio modulation
the big sound from underground anotha pirate station
we bring the truth to places truth is never heard before
we bring the sound communication of our tribal war
dark vision fly by helicopters in the night
attempt triangulation of our station in the fight
straight from the bass the deep down low precision
high crime treason we broadcastin' sedission
like the wall street mornin afternoon edition
commandeering airwaves from unknown positions

        (chorus)
Live and direct we comin never pre-recorded
with information that will never be reported
disregard the mainstream media distorted
whoop! whoop!
we comin' listener supported

        (repeat)

Don't take no prisoners if you can't afford to feed none
don't start no fights if you cannot predict the outcome
don't make donations where you cannot get your dough back
fuck the apathetic bullshittas send 'em all your Prozac
I will not climb into your telephone tree
and "Hell no you can't put put me on hold!!!"
"Hell no!!!!!"
it's same recorded message you been singin' all along
keep on handin' us the bible while you walkin' off with the gold
the bureaucratic office sends you merry go rounding
while the KKK police the streets by blood hounding
interest on the credit card just keeps on compounding
but the FCC can neva shut this pirate sound down pirate sound down

        (chorus)

Third Annual 911/Power to the Peaceful Festival.
Dolores Park, San Francisco, 2001

SKIN ON THE DRUM

I was born botanical
the soul of an animal
deep beneath the layers, I sink my roots,
no need for mechanical
come strictly organical
when I need to feast, I look to the East
that's why I'm never scared of the beast
even though they try to prey upon me
I'm protected by the one always greater than me
so now I reveal to thee
because you wanna see
the contour of my mystery
strength of my arches
the color of my conscience
and the way that I process my diction
some fact some fiction some memory
and some future fantasy
I'm the trunk that holds the branches
the leaves who do the dances
my flowers romantic
and my love is gigantic
from Africa, transplanted transatlantic
in the heat of the sun
I bring shade for everyone
like the beat on the one
I'm the skin on the drum

   (chorus)
I keep on living with the fullness of the one
like the heat of the sun or the skin on the drum

See I been full marinated now I'm ready for the fire
so you can fire now!!!!
fire one!!!
fire two....!!!

See now I'm fully marinated
and now I'm ready for the fire
see I'm beginning to perspire
from deep within to the skin
yo, the feminine and the masculine
the pieces of the puzzle
see me reflections in the puddle
after the storm the purple of the sky
brings to mind another time
when we resided
below the water line
life was fine there human, divine
but in the years following
evil men came, swallowing
everything in sight
some learned to run, some stayed to fight
I kneeled at the tomb of the soldier
said I would love to behold her
the magic in store there
she touched me on the shoulder
she said," in time all is revealed, box of light be unsealed...
...now listen to me son, be like the skin on the drum."

   (chorus)
I'm fully marinated now I'm ready for the fire
so you can fire now!!!!
fire one!!!
fire two....!!!

And as all the pepper gas clears
and police and protesters go home
just as the morning dew are tear drops of the night,
my emotions are always there for you.
And will never leave you dry...Bless....

Songs from the Front Porch

2002

LISTEN IN TO MY stethoscope
on a rope
internal lullaby's human cries
~~Algon cataclysmic~~
THUMPS AND SILENCE
THE LANGUAGE OF VIOLENCE
ALGORHYTHMIC cataclysmic seismic
BIORhythmic
you can make a LIFE LONGER BUT
you cant save it.
YOU can make a clone then you try to enslave
stealin' DNA SAMPLES from the unborn
then you comin after us cuz we sample
a James BROWN HORN
SCIENTISTS whose God is Progress
A FOUR Headed sheep is there latest Project
CIA RUNNIN Like that Jones from
INdiana killin' people like that Jones
IN GUYANA
WAW IT AINT NO CARTOON
NO ONE SLIPS ON BANANAS
DO YOU Reall THINK THAT CAR KILLED
DIANA
HELL, I SHOT RONAL REGAN
I SHOT JFK I SLEPT WITH M.M.
AND SHE SANG ME HAPPY B-DAY

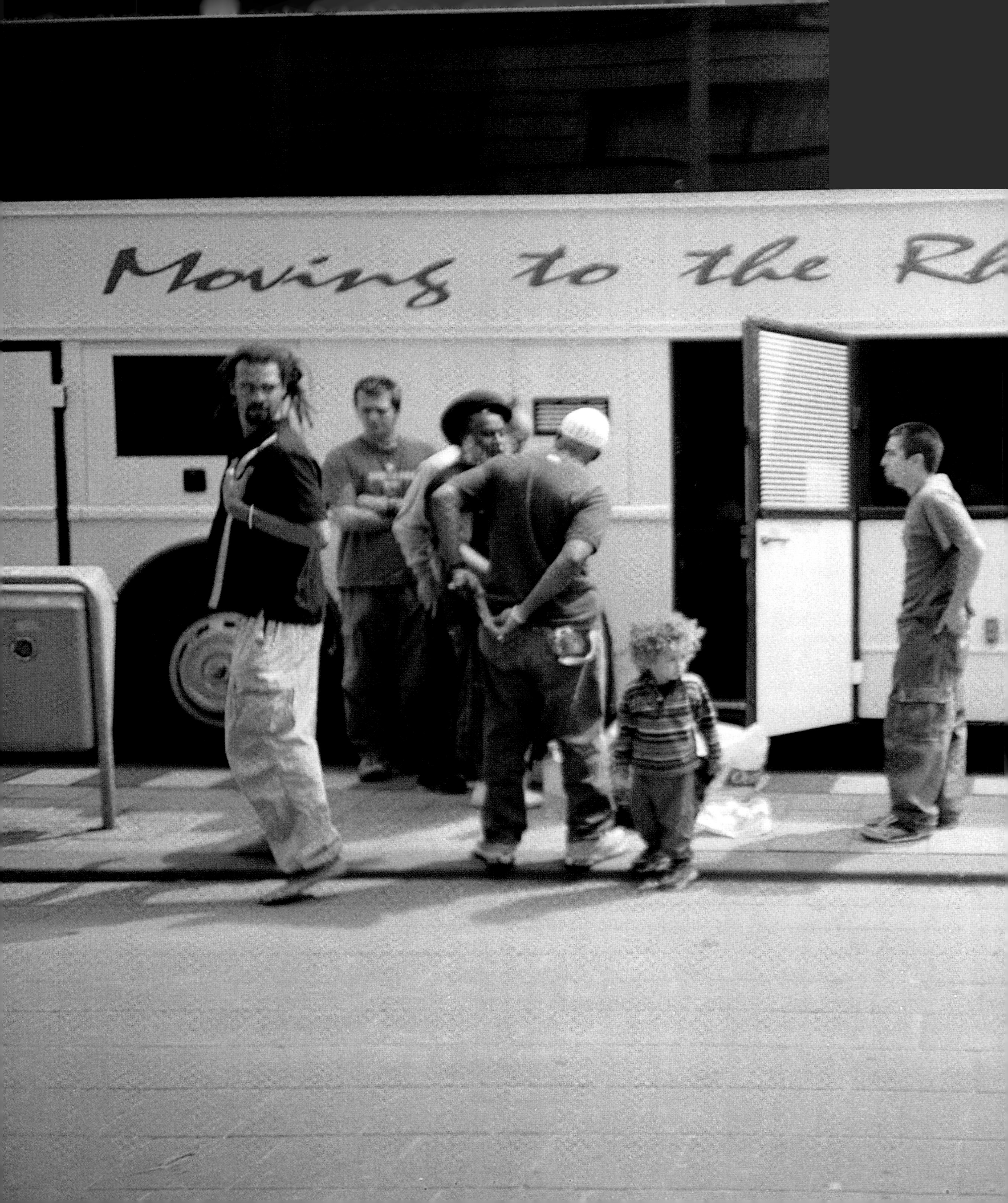
Moving to the Rh

FIREFLY

I'll be your firefly
shinin' bright
when dark clouds
come across the sky

I'll be your firefly
so you can see
your way to me
at midnight
you'll be my firefly
burnin' flames

Incinerate
a path for me

And that is why
I'm not afraid
to go at night
to see my firefly

Burn baby burn
burn baby burn! burn! baby
burn burn baby burn
like a sweet glow worm!!!

*(previous page) Original draft of
"Oh My God" which was
included on the 2002 Boo Boo Wax
release,* Songs From the Front
Porch, *which was an acoustic
collection of songs from previous
albums as well as several
unreleased songs*

(opposite) Getting off the bus in Rotterdam, Holland, 2001

CLOSER TO THE SKY

I'm so very happy just to be here
I'm so glad I'm finally in a space with you
people say that we should never do this
but they don't, they don't wanna know the truth

You can try, you can try
to build a fortress in your mind
try to stack up all your things so high
you can try, you can try
to climb away from this life
but it will only bring you closer to the sky
People say that you should never come here
something bad is only gonna happen to you
better stay inside where we can see you
if you don't we'll make sure that you're feeling blue

You can try, you can try
to build a fortress in your mind
try to stack up all your things so high
you can try, you can try
to climb away from this life
but it will only bring you closer to the sky

Some people think that life is worth living for tomorrow
some people think that life is worth living for today
some people think that life is worth nothing but sorrow
some people think that life is worth living day by day

We can try, we can try
to build a fortress in your mind
try to stack up all your things so high
we can try, we can try
to climb away from this life
but it will only bring us closer to the sky

Sugar cane fields, Maui, 2000.
Photo by Tara Rye

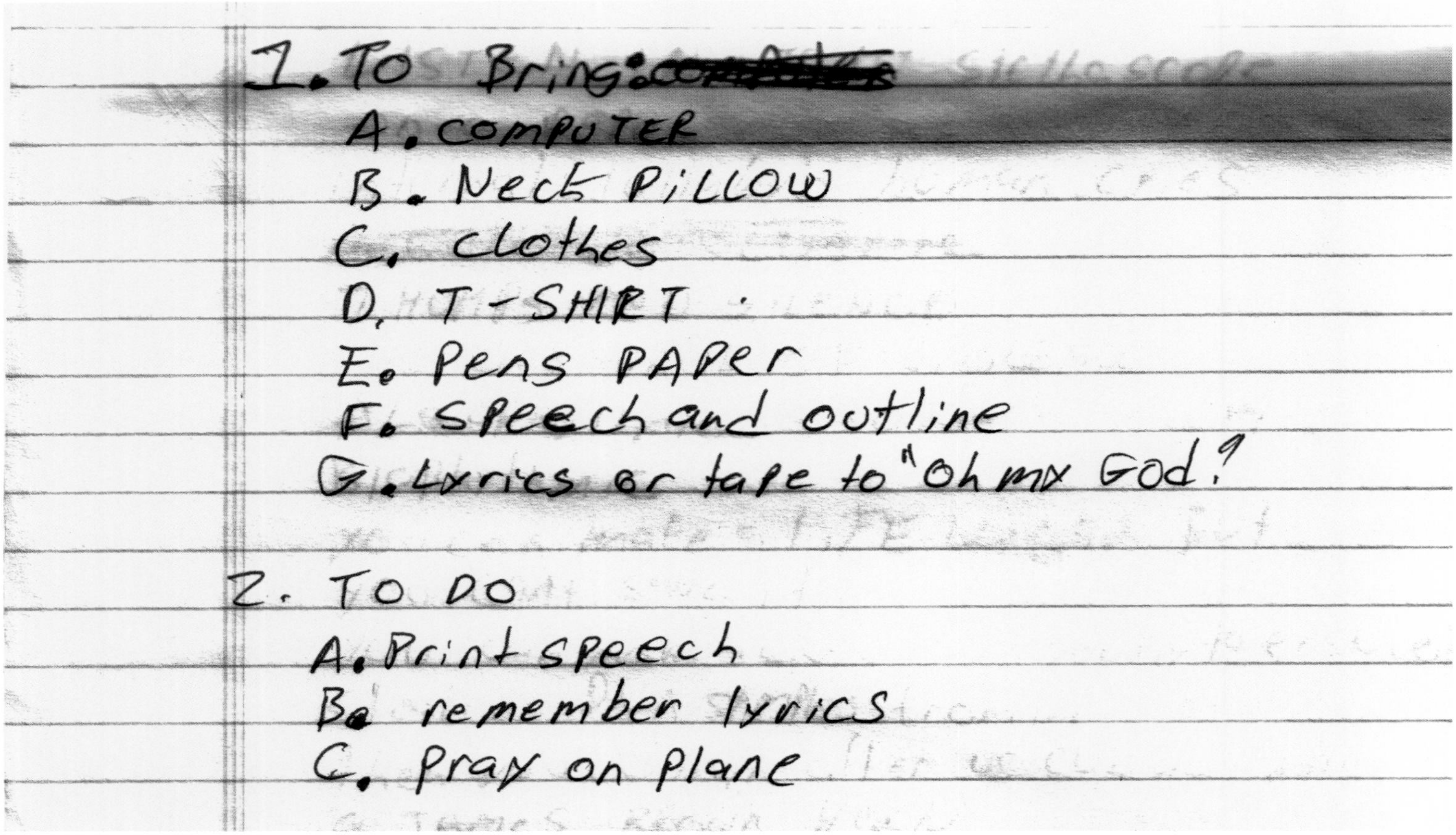

1. TO Bring: ~~computer~~
   A. COMPUTER
   B. Neck Pillow
   C. clothes
   D. T-SHIRT
   E. Pens PAPer
   F. Speech and outline
   G. Lyrics or tape to "Oh my God?"

2. TO DO
   A. Print speech
   B. remember lyrics
   C. pray on plane

(above) Michael does most of his writing and planning on large yellow legal notepads. Here is a to-do list used before heading to the airport to for a speaking engagement at the University of Mississippi. Michael never got on the flight as all flights were cancelled that morning. 2001

Michael Performing at Berbati's Pan on Valentine's Day, Portland, Oregon, 2000

ANYBODY SEEN MY MIND

Everybody wants to be who they wanna be
everybody wants to have a good time
I just want a peaceful little bit of family
playin' sweet sweet music with some friends of mine

But I try hard to fake it but I can't do it all the time
I tried hard to break it but it was just a waste of my time
when I turn on my tv seems they're winnin' all the time
so I pray to God to please show me a sign
has anybody seen my mind?
has anybody seen my mind?
I know I ain't seen you around here in a long long time
but have you seen my mind?

I would never leave you hangin' on the corner with a problem
I would never leave you all alone
I always wanted you to know that you can depend on me
and when I come out to your place
I will never ever be without a home

    (chorus)

EVERYONE
DESERVES MUSIC

2003

CRAZY CRAZY CRAZY

SHINE ON ALL MY PEOPLE
WHO BEEN BROKEN HEARTED
SHINE ON FROM THE PLACE WHERE
ALL LIFE HAS BEEN STARTED
WHEN YOU NEED FRESH AIR GO
BEYOND HORIZONS TO YOUR PLACE
IN THE SUN, SHINE ON! LET YOUR
HEART BE BOUNDLESS LIKE YOUR
FAITH IN THE ONE!

IT'S CRAZY, CRAZY, CRAZY
DONT TELL ME THAT YOU DONT CARE

NO STOPPING TO THIS WARFARE

WE'RE BREATHING IN THE SAME AIR

SOMEBODY PLEASE SEND US A PRAYER

WHAT I BE

If I could be the sun
I'd radiate like Africa and
smile upon the world
intergalactic love laughter and
if I were the rains, I'd wash away the whole world's pain and
bring the gift of cool like ice cream trucks on sunny days and
if I were the earth I'd be like mountains bountiful
and If I were the sky so high, I'd be like wind invincible and
if I could be a seed, I would give birth to redwood trees and
if I were the trees, I'd generate the freshest air to breathe in

     (chorus)
What I be, is what I be
what I be, is what I be
and on and on and on
on and on and on

And I say
well, well, well, movin' on!
well, well, well, movin' on!
do you love someone? Do you love somebody?
then hold that one!
love someone!

If I could be the leaves, like jade I would stay evergreen and
spread my limbs out wide and pull love so close to me and
if I could be the roots, I would dig deep like ancestry and
if I were the fruits, you'd make the sweetest cherry pie for me and
if I could be the night, my moon replace all 'lectric lights and
magic music would transmit from outer space on satellites
if myself could be the ocean, you would feel emotion all the time and
if I were the words, then everything that everybody said would rhyme

     (chorus)

If I could be sex my word would protect
I'd be in the lives of all who connect
what the heck, I'd make it so we all got selected
pores would be dripping pure hot intellect and
the minds of the masses would all stay erect and
then just for kicks, I'd mail out some checks
addressed to those who sent their used latex in
yes, that's what I would do if I were sex
if I could be you, and you could be me
I could be you, you could be me
I could walk a mile in your shoes...
and you could walk a mile in my bare feet

     (chorus)

WE DON'T STOP

They got a war for oil, a war for gold
a war for money and a war for souls
a war on terror, a war on drugs
a war on kindness, a war on hugs
a war on birds and a war on bees
they got a war on hippies tryin'a save the trees
a war with jets and a war with missiles
a war with high-seated government officials
Wall Street war on high finance
a war on people who just love to dance
a war on music, a war on speech
a war on teachers and the things they teach
a war for the last 500 years
war's just messin' up the atmosphere
a war on Muslims, a war on Jews

We can't stop it with the rebel rock!
and we don't stop
we can't stop 'till we hit those heights!
and we don't stop
we can't stop 'cause we love this life!

Dance to the new day
Sing to the new day, rhyme to the new day
Transform hell into heaven god lives through
Grab hold of today
Yesterday is over, tomorrow may be too late
Everything is one, but the one is off balance
Music made for the dollar like soul and talent
Really ain't it all about a feeling you was havin'
As a child runnin' wild

a war on Christians and Hindus
a whole lotta people sayin' kill them all
they gotta war on Mumia Abu Jamal
the war on pot is a war that's failed
a war that's fillin' up the nation's jails
World War one, two three and four
chemical weapons, biological war
Bush war one and bush war two
they gotta war for me, they gotta war for you!

(chorus)
We can't stop it when the beat just drops!
and we don't stop

before the mind programmin' set in
threatenin' your establishment
get in this energy, lay back and sit
the next men wreckin', to the master's lips
head spin brethren, get to askin' if
where, when Mr. President, "What do you know?"
it's evident settin' in slow, "How does it go?"

An unprecedented event is about to unfold
the devil can't stop, won't stop blockin' the globe
fall in a cell here
freedom come knock at the door
they try lockin' it, through, but we about to explode
we got the firefly, tiger eye apocalypse flow

so deep in the bottom of your bottomless soul
send mind darts flyin' out, without a pistol
redesign lost minds got outta the cold
bring order to a world that is outta control
"truth" you say, I say "How do I know?"

(chorus)

I wanna rock with punks because I love punk rock
I wanna rock with heads because I love hip-hop
I wanna rock my beats all around the block
if I was in Baghdad then I would rock Iraq
I wanna rock with punks because I love punk rock
I wanna rock with heads because I love hip-hop
I wanna rock my beats all around the block

new world beats for the new world to bang
new world streets for the new world to hang
new world president, new world drugs
new world president, new world thugs
new world players for the new world sports
new world trials for the new world courts
new world lawyers and new world laws
new world prisons and new world bars
new world fight the new world's fists

The new world lighting up the new world spliffs
new world smoke in the new world lungs
new world's choking, the new world's done

(chorus)

Michael gives an interview in a Stockholm, Sweden hotel during the release of Stay Human, *2001*

there is just one love, so the planet we rock
new world days and new world nights
new world wrongs and new world rights

Putting new world funds in the new world banks
with the new world guns on the new world tanks
new world devils and new world gods
new world jails, see the new world's hard
new world names sing new world songs
new world planes are the new world bombs
new world's flying, the new world's dying
the new world's crying and the new world's trying
new world sons and new world daughters
they're already selling us new world water

EVERYONE DESERVES MUSIC

Everyone deserves music, sweet music
everyone deserves music, sweet music

Seven in the morn', step on the floor
walk into the kitchen and you open the door
ain't much left in the bottle of juice
because the seeds that you planted never reproduced
computer still runnin'
but your mind has crashed
because the plans that you made never came to pass
now you recognizin' the times is hard
when you tryin'a take a bite out your ATM card

   (chorus)
Everyone deserves music, sweet music
everyone deserves music, sweet music
even our worst enemies, Lord, they deserve music, music
and even the quiet ones in our family, they deserve music

Ginny's home wouldn't stabilize
at the age of fifteen learned to drink and drive
no one could ever seem to empathize
makin' babies in the back seat on tranquilizers
Papa never was much of a rolling stone see
he just liked to sit and drink alone
Mama always tried to do the best she could
she would work all day
and come home to cook but
we all vain, we all strange
we all stained, we all love to just complain
but nobody wants to seem to get along, ya see
we got shame, we got pain
we got blame, we all a little bit insane
so that's why I sing this song, y'know, because

   (chorus)

So I pray for them, and I'll play for them
so I pray for them and I'll play for them
we all vain, we all strange
we all drained, we all love to just complain
but nobody wants to seem to get along, ya see
we got shame, we got pain
we got blame, we all a little bit insane
so that's why I sing this song, y'know, because

   (chorus)

*Michael listens to Carl's new bass groove backstage at
Palookaville. Santa Cruz, CA, 2000*

Never Too Late

Don't fear your best friends
because a best friend would never try to do ya wrong
and don't fear your worst friends
because a worst friends' just a best friend that's done ya wrong
don't fear the nighttime, no
because the monsters know that you're divine
and don't fear the sunshine
'cause everything is better in the summer time
summer time

(chorus)
And it's never to late to start the day over
never too late to pick up the phone
pick up the phone and call me
it's never too late to lay your head down on my shoulders
it's never too late to come on home
come on home

Don't fear the water
'cause you can swim inside you within your skin
don't fear your father
'cause a father's just a boy without a friend
and don't fear to walk slow
don't be a horse race, be a marathon
and don't fear the long road
'cause on the long road, you gotta long time to sing a simple song
sing along

(chorus)

Don't fear your teachers
'cause if you listen, you can hear music in the school bell
don't fear your preacher
if he can't find heaven in a prison cell
don't fear your own self
payin' money to justify your worth
and don't fear your family
because you chose them a long time before your birth
yes you did

(chorus)

Hold to your children
hold to your children
hold to your children
let 'em know
let 'em know
let 'em know

Michael and his son, Cappy. San Francisco, 2003

BOMB THE WORLD

Please tell me the reason
behind the colors that you fly
love just one nation
and the whole world we divide
you say you're sorry
it's no other choice
but God bless the people now
who cannot raise their voice

(chorus)
We can chase down all our enemies
bring them to their knees
we can bomb the world to pieces
but we can't bomb it into peace
whoa, we may even find a solution
to hunger and disease
we can bomb the world to pieces
but we can't bomb it into peace

Violence brings one thing
more, more of the same
military madness
the smell of flesh and burning pain
so I sing out to the masses
stand up if you're still sane!
to all of us gone crazy
I sing this one refrain

(chorus)

And I sing
power to the peaceful
love to the peaceful, y'all
I sing
power to the peaceful
love to the peaceful, y'all

Michael develops the chords for "Bomb the World" before
recording one of seven versions of the song during the
making of the album Everyone Deserves Music. *Two*
versions (the album version and the Armageddon Re-Mix)
eventually made it on to the finished album.
The Sugar Shack, San Francisco, 2002

PRAY FOR GRACE

Why must I feel like this today?
I'm a soldier but afraid sometimes
to face the things that may
block the sun from shinin' rays
and fill my life with shades of gray
but still I long to find a way
so today I pray for grace

and I'll be dead for a million more after I'm gone
so I live to give somethin'
that can live on
like the way you hum a song
when the music's gone
like the warmth of the sand
when the sun goes down

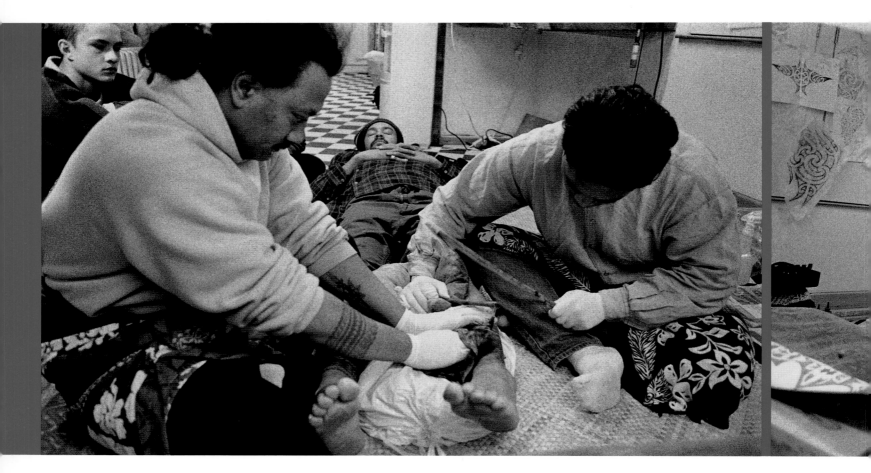

I take a moment to myself
so I can heal myself
to feel myself and be real myself
life's addictions and afflictions
cause abrasions from their friction
sometimes it's easier to live in fiction

I can run, but I can't hide
from the pains that reside down deep inside
there is no pill that can be swallowed
there is no guru that can be followed
there's no escapin' from my own history
those that I hurt and those that hurt me
I was dead for a million years 'fore I was born

and I'm sittin' with myself
nobody else is around but

(chorus)

It's been a long, long time
since I been away
been a long, long time
since I felt this way
been a long, long time
I found the words to say
how much I'm grateful for my life today
'cause under every cup you might find a nut
behind every corner you might get jacked up

At the end of every rainbow you might find gold
the last bite of your sandwich, hope you don't find mold
'cause none of us can live the perfect life
the kind that we see on Nick at Night
and sometimes we all just lose sight
of the pain that will guide us

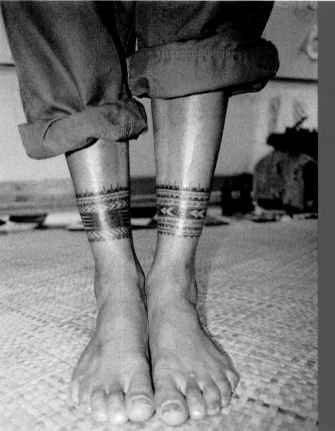

Michael receives Samoan tattoos, using traditional hand tools. Moko Ink Auckland, New Zealand, 2001

from dark into the light
we fall down, yes, but we get up
and sometimes we just need a little bit o' love
to help to make it through another day
into the night, into the light, into a Saturday
so in the mornin' when I've waitin' for the sun to raise
and my head's a little foggy
like I'm in a haze
I remind myself that everything is gonna be okay
I take a breath, slow down and say...

    (chorus)

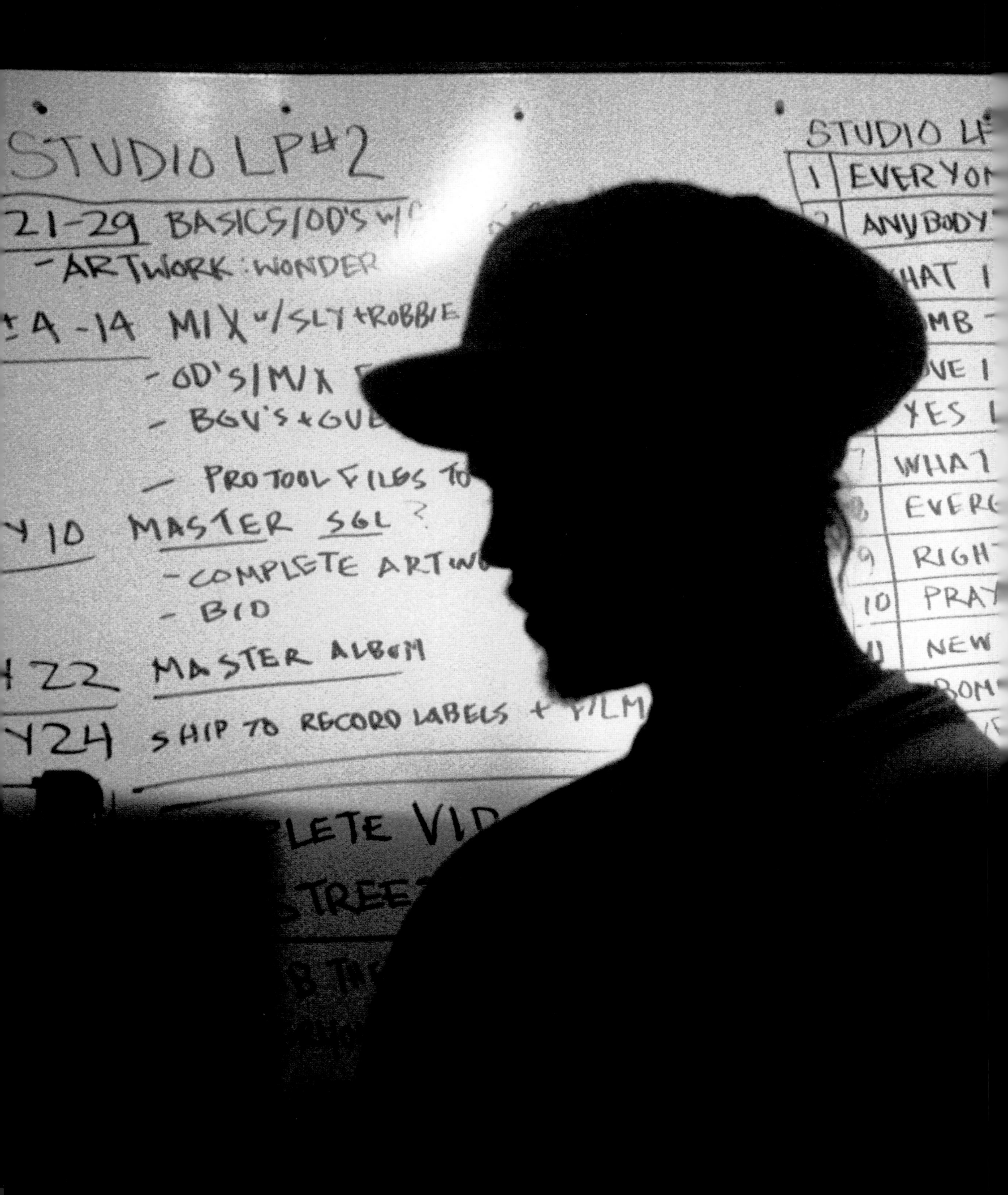

STUDIO LP#2

21-29 BASICS/OD'S w/

- ARTWORK : WONDER

±4-14 MIX w/ SLY +ROBBIE

    - OD'S/MIX

    - BGV'S + GUE

    - PRO TOOL FILES TO

Y 10 MASTER SGL ?

    - COMPLETE ARTW

    - BIO

±22 MASTER ALBUM

Y24 SHIP TO RECORD LABELS + FILM

...LETE VID

...TREE

...8 TA

STUDIO L

1	EVERYO
2	ANYBODY
	...HAT I
	...MB -
	...VE I
	YES I
7	WHAT
8	EVER
9	RIGH
10	PRAY
11	NEW
	...OM

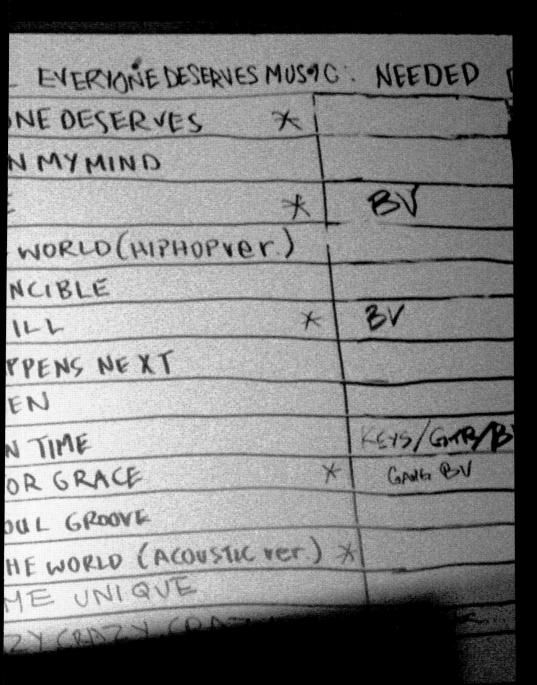

EVERYONE DESERVES MUSIC: NEEDED

ONE DESERVES ✗

N MY MIND

✗ | BV

WORLD (HIPHOP ver.)

NCIBLE

ILL ✗ | BV

PPENS NEXT

EN

N TIME | KEYS/GTR/B

OR GRACE ✗ | GANG BV

OUL GROOVE

HE WORLD (ACOUSTIC ver.) ✗

ME UNIQUE

ZY CRAZY

LOVE, WHY DID YOU GO AWAY?

Love
why did you have to go away?
leave us here all alone
to survive these crazy, crazy days

And love
see we been really missin' you
some new times have come now
seems like we've forgotten you

(chorus)
But we wanted you to know
we never wanted you to go
and we wanted you to know
we never wanted you to go

Love
why did you leave us here alone?
when we dropped bombs upon each other
picked up guns and we shot our brothers
when dad got drunk and yelled at mother
where were you?
I said where were you?

(chorus)

Love
where were you when we were scared?
when no one shared?
no one cared?
when we chopped down the final tree
broke apart the human family
so now I'm beggin' you today
I know it was us who ran away

(chorus)

Never ever ever ever wanted you to go away now...

Michael's silhouette in front of the huge dry erase chalkboard at the Sugar Shack. On the board is a list of songs in progress for the album Everyone Deserves Music. *The songs listed that were not used on the album go into the "vaults" to be revisited for later projects. San Francisco, 2002*

YES I WILL

I received the letter that you wrote me
on a dark, cold and cloudy day
remindin' me, on the side of the road
you find the light, you'll find a friend
you'll find a way
but today I'm feelin' all broke down
I ain't got the faintest clue about what to do
can't comprehend the situation at hand
so I try my best just to get back home to you

    (chorus)
Gonna keep on walkin' now
yes I will
gonna keep on talkin' loud
yes I will
gonna keep on singin' 'bout it
yes I will
gonna keep on ringin' out
yes I will

I believe that what you sing to the clouds
will rain upon you when your sun has gone away
and I believe that what you dream to the moon
will manifest before you rest another day
so stay strong and sleep long when you need to
let the mornin' take you right on through the day
when you find you're at the end of the road
you just lift your head up
spread your wings and fly away

    (chorus)

When you're lost and alone
that's when the rainbow comes
when you're lost and alone
that's when the rainbow comes for you

Michael carries his son Ade' down a secluded
street in Milano, Italy, 2001

FEELIN' FREE

I wanna thank you
for the seeds you've planted in me
and I wanna thank you
for the earth that roots my feet
I wanna thank you
for the sun that greens my leaves
and I say I wanna thank you for the mystery, mystery

> *(chorus)*
> *But it seems to me*
> *that I'm about to be*
> *feelin' free now*
> *take a bow when you feel like a superstar*
> *shake your pants*
> *when you show what you feel inside your heart*
> *throw your hands in the air*
> *when you feel like love is your need*
> *when you can't feel a thing just hold onto me*

Please remember me
when I close my eyes
please remember me
when I scream my silent cries
will you remember me
when I'm not doin' my best?
will you remember me
when my spirit needs to rest?

> *(chorus)*

*Michael runs down the street a few blocks from his home in
Hunter's Point, San Francisco, 2001*

LOVE INVINCIBLE

When I fall down
I need a helpin' hand
and when I lose my head
it's 'cause it's buried in the sand
when I get stuck on myself
feelin' sorry for myself
will you help me grab a hold?
and please don't patronize my soul
when I start to lose control
when I get irrational
when I start to get too high
and you see me come floatin' by, I say...

(chorus)
Touch me in the mornin' sun
when I feel impossible
show me what is possible
teach me love invincible
touch me in the mornin' sun
when I feel impossible
show me what is possible
teach me love invincible

When you're down
you need a helpin' hand
and when you lose your head
I'll help you wash away the sand
and when you get stuck on yourself
feelin' sorry for yourself
I will help you grab a hold and
I won't patronize your soul
when you start to lose control
when you get irrational
when you start to get too high
I see you come floatin' by, I'll say...

(chorus)

And when we're down
we need a helpin' hand
and when we lose our heads
it's 'cause they're buried in the sand
and when we get stuck on ourselves
feelin' sorry for ourselves
will you help us grab a hold?
and please don't patronize our souls
when we start to lose control
when we get irrational
when we start to get to high
and you see us come floatin' by, I say...

(chorus)

Michael on the bus on the way to Mountain Aire
Music Festival, Angel's Camp CA, 2000

BOMB THE WORLD (ARMAGEDDON VERSION)

I don't understand the whole reason why
you tellin' us all that we need to unify
rally 'round the flag
and beat the drums of war
sing the same old songs
we heard 'em all before
you tellin' me it's unpatriotic
but I call it what I see it
when I see it's idiotic
the tears of one mother
are the same as any other
drop food on the kids
while you're murderin' their fathers
but don't bother to show it on CNN
brothers and sisters don't believe them
that it's a war against evil
it's really just revenge
engaged on the poorest by the same rich men
fight terrorists wherever they be found
but why you not bombing Tim McVeigh's hometown?
you can say what you want, propaganda television
but all bombing is terrorism

   (chorus)
We can chase down all our enemies
we can bring them to their knees
we can bomb the world to pieces
but we can't bomb it into peace
whoa, we may even find a solution
to hunger and disease
we can bomb the world to pieces
but we can't bomb it into peace

9/11
fire in the skies
many people died
no one even really knows why
they tellin' lies of division and fear

we yelled and cried
no one listened for years
but like, "Who put us here?"
and who's responsible?
well, there's no debatin'
'cause if they ask me I say
it's big corporations
world trade organization
trilateral action
international sanctions, satan
seems like it'll be an endless price tag
of wars tremendous
and most disturbingly
the death toll is so horrendous
so I send this to those
who say they defend us
send us into harm's way
we should all make a remembrance that
this is bigger than terrorism
blood is blood is blood and um,
love is true vision
who will listen?
how many songs it takes for you to see
you can bomb the world to pieces
you can't bomb it into peace

(chorus)

And I sing
power to the peaceful
and I sing
love to the peaceful, y'all
I sing
power to the peaceful
and I sing
love to the peaceful, y'all

(chorus)

Michael, Sly Dunbar, Carl Young and Robbie
Shakespeare at the Sugar Shack, San Francisco, 2002

CRAZY, CRAZY, CRAZY

Shine on
all my people who been broken-hearted
Shine on
from the place where all life had been started
when you need fresh air
go beyond horizons to your place in the sun
Shine on
let your heart be boundless like your faith in the one

(chorus)
It's crazy, crazy, crazy
don't tell me that you don't care
It's crazy crazy, crazy
no stoppin' of this warfare
It's crazy, crazy, crazy
we're breathing in the same air
It's crazy, crazy, crazy
don't tell me that you don't care

Sing on
from the language of your ancestors and
sing on
be playful in your innocence and
lift your head up high
and rejoice for all you see without your eyes
sing on
like a bird that's making love in sunset skies

(chorus)

No life's worth more than any other
no sister worthless than any brother

(chorus)

.. somebody please send us a prayer!

Michael performing in Auckland, Aotearoa (New Zealand), 2001